I0644014

Son Hong-kyu

The Muslim Butcher

a novel

Son Hong-kyu

The Muslim Butcher

a novel

Translated by Yu Young-nan

MERWIN
MA
ASIA

MerwinAsia
Portland, Maine

MERWIN
MA
ASIA

Copyright © 2016 by MerwinAsia

The Muslim Butcher
Islam Chŏngyukjŏm

Copyright © 2010 by Son Hongkyu

English translation Copyright © 2016 by Yu Young-nan

All rights reserved. No part of this book may be reproduced in any form without written permission from the publisher, MerwinAsia

59 West St., Unit 3W,
Portland, ME 04102 USA
www.merwinasia.com

The Muslim Butcher is published under the support of Literature Translation Institute of Korea (LTI Korea).

Distributed by the University of Hawai'i Press

Library of Congress Control Number: 2016910834

ISBN 978-1-937385-41-5 (Paperback)
ISBN 978-1-937385-42-2 (Hardcover)

Printed in the United States of America

The paper used in this publication meets the minimum requirements of the American National Standard for Information Services—Permanence of Paper for Printed Library Materials,
ANSI/NISO Z39/48-1992

Book and Cover Design: Lucian Burg, Lu Design Studios
www.ludesignstudios.com

Son Hong-kyu

The Muslim Butcher

a novel

1

My adoptive father's blood is flowing in my body.

It was Uncle Hassan, my adoptive father, who told me the meaning of Islam: submission, *sunjong* in Korean. He seemed apprehensive when people asked him questions. He looked all the more uneasy if they came from a boy like me, whose face and scalp were marred with ringworm scars. When I asked him something, however, I sensed that he was secretly pleased. As I stared at him with eyes sparkling with curiosity, he seemed nervous as he grumpily spat out an answer and then pursed his lips. It would be unnecessary to add that his expression was far from being submissive when he said, "It means submission."

Uncle Amos described Uncle Hassan as a guy "who was kicking as he left his mother's womb." He meant that Uncle Hassan couldn't be further from the word "submission." From the first day I met him, Uncle Hassan was the emblem of non-submission. He behaved as though he were deaf. I mean, he didn't pay any attention to what people were saying. He handled me roughly as though I were a marionette. Whenever his hand touched me, I got a feeling that I was deciphering a book written in an unfamiliar script.

When Uncle Hassan said, it means submission, Aunt Anna

snorted as she was wont to do. Aunt Anna, charming at times but mostly cursed, would sprinkle in proverbs as she spoke, the sayings new to me, not to mention to Uncle Hassan and Uncle Amos. When I used rough words like "damn" or "I fucking lost face," her goat-like eyes welled up with tears at lightning speed and she made a fuss as if she were seeing a devil that had just dropped from the sky. She wrapped me up in her thick arms, smothering me in her doughy breasts, and, putting her garlic-redolent mouth close to my ear, whispered a mantra.

She habitually recited *Om Mani Padme Hum,* but when I showed my curiosity about its meaning, she reddened and stammered, "What meaning can there be in a saying that has been handed down forever, from generation to generation?" Then she spilled out a litany of proverbs that I gathered to mean "ignorance is bliss." Her anger dissipated by then, she slapped me on the bottom and burst into merry laughter. Her laughter made me believe that it'd be impossible for anyone to hate her unless he was out of his mind.

Later in life, I had an opportunity to tell her that *Om Mani Padme Hum* signified "jewel in the lotus," symbolizing none other than the Buddha. I expected she'd look grossly offended and pretend to be cross, claiming she'd known it all along—"Did you think I didn't know a basic thing like that?"—as she used to do. But instead of fibbing, she seemed greatly moved. She embraced me just like when I was a boy and shed a quiet tear. "You're the first person who taught me something like that," she said.

Aunt Anna reacted in a huff to Uncle Hassan's terse explanation—submission—because she assumed he was throwing the word at her. Uncle Hassan was from a country where it was all right to have two wives, even three or four if men could afford them. This alone was enough reason for her to hold him in disdain. She decided he must have been a playboy and mightily regretted that at their first encounter she hadn't thrown salt over his shoulder to ward off evil spirits.

"Polygamy in this day and age?" she'd say. "Are they even human? They're no better than sea lions!"

She often brought up sea lions after she saw a seal show at a zoo where she went with Uncle Amos, and was impressed, for some reason, by the explanation that the performing seals were actually sea lions. She must also have been impressed by the fact that a male sea lion had several wives at his command, just like men in Uncle Hassan's country. For some time after her visit to the zoo, she often tossed around phrases like "a guy like a sea lion" or "a fellow like a sea lion" as part of her figurative speech.

When she was worked up, it posed an obstacle for Uncle Amos. According to her, he was "a guy who snores loudly when he's squatting at someone else's place," by which she meant that he, her tenant, was inconsiderate and behaved like a landlord. When Uncle Amos craned his neck and peered into her restaurant from the doorway, it might take half an hour or an hour, but usually he was fed.

"I want to make it clear that I've rented a room, not taken in a boarder," she complained every single time, but she fed him all the same. He worked as an orderly in the laundry of a general hospital. When he had time to spare, he helped out at a funeral parlor. Still, he was always hungry. Aunt Anna understood his circumstances better than anyone else did. When she was carried away, however, his mendicant tactics didn't work. She would forget that she was about to feed him.

"What are you doing, standing there?" While saying this, she intended to feed him, but soon forgot about it. It was because her thoughts strayed. In short, Uncle Amos might be fed or not, depending on her mood. His joints creaked as he walked, just like unoiled machinery. At the particular time I'm talking about, he lurched toward me in that very gait and poked me in the side. He was prompting me to join forces with Aunt Anna on her offensive against Uncle Hassan.

I ventured, "I know a boy. His name is Sunjong, 'submission.'

He's the pastor's son at Happiness Church. He must be a Muslim, too. Don't you think?"

Uncle Hassan's thick eyebrows wiggled, an indication of displeasure.

Aunt Anna was always tickled pink to see Uncle Hassan's wiggling eyebrows. She said this was as good as watching a comedy skit. Anyone, before getting used to her ways, would assume that her mental maturation had stopped at puberty. I mean, she would come off as brazen. But what an adorable woman she was! I'd never met anyone who made more delicious kimchi than she did. Her hands, after a bit of tossing and kneading, transformed any droopy, wilted greens into palatable side dishes. When her hand, with four hard nubs embedded just like chewy cartilage in sliced pork belly, touched my burning brow, my fever subsided. When her hand rubbed my upset stomach, cold knots inside me went away. When she blew on my scraped knee after I tripped on the steep slope leading to the mosque, I felt it was half healed.

Even Uncle Amos, who was stingy with compliments, said she was Gaea. Aunt Anna, not knowing that Gaea refers to Mother Earth, stopped feeding him, with a ruthlessness equal to a dictator's who'd just staged a successful coup. So, Uncle Amos lifted me up to the Temple of Olympus and repeated his supplication for my intervention.

Had I not borrowed a copy of *Greek-Roman Mythology* from the neighborhood library and showed it to Aunt Anna, her meal suspension would have lasted longer. Actually, it wasn't me but the anonymous illustrator for whom Uncle Amos had to be thankful. The illustrator must have been passionately in love when he drew Gaea; he depicted her as more opulent and steamy than Venus, the goddess of beauty. Aunt Anna's mouth split from ear to ear, as her pet expression went. "So this is me, huh? Gaea sounded like a gay or something, but this is really me, he says!"

She tore off the illustrated page and taped it next to a wanted poster distributed by the police. Her customers cast cursory glances at the illustration, but she studied it whenever she had a spare moment. "Lots of people said I looked like Bodhisattva, but it's the first time I hear I'm like a goddess, Gaea or whatever her name is." She dabbed her eyes with her apron. She was moved because she was admired as a foreign goddess, not just any run-of-the-mill native deity. Gaea stayed up there for a long time until it was stained with kimchi juice splattered by some careless customer and a ballpoint-pen moustache was drawn in.

As for me, I agreed with Uncle Amos. It wasn't a stretch to call Aunt Anna Mother Earth. Many people who remember her, although most of them are dead now, haven't forgotten the miracle I'm going to describe.

Her restaurant was located on a steep side road that was barely wide enough for a single car to pass by. One day, on that road, a group of young men got into a violent scuffle. One of them, who'd been a favored customer of Aunt Anna's, crawled to her doorstep, a hand pressing his slashed abdomen and a rivulet of thick blood trickling through his fingers. Aunt Anna, seized with an ominous premonition, shoved open her sliding front door to take a look outside. "It was odd. I felt a chill running through me, like right before a storm," she would say later. The day was clear, without a speck of cloud. The neighbors, too frightened to venture out, had been watching the fight from their shops, by the windows of their second-story homes, or from their attics, and saw Aunt Anna helping the man up and taking him inside. A little later, when his dark red blood, snaking around the stones strewn on the road, was mixed with clumps of dust and congealed like jelly, they saw him leaving the restaurant as if nothing had happened, his small, fair-complexioned face lit up with a broad smile. Like a son going off to work, he lifted his arm high to wave at Aunt Anna, with his palm stained with old blood like a rusty sheet of iron, and strode off toward St. Mary's Hospital. He walked into the emergency room and died there thirty minutes later.

Later in life, I surmised that he'd experienced a flash of lucidity.

Excruciating physical pain often erodes consciousness, pushing us to delirium, but at times it alerts our brain, ushering in a state that is sharper and calmer than any other time. He must have needed Aunt Anna's voice, breath, and gaze, so much so that he forgot about his physical pain for a while. But then who wouldn't have needed her caring presence?

In the days leading to my departure from the orphanage with Uncle Hassan, I was violent, as most frightened people tend to be as a way to cope with their fear. But the only object I could inflict violence on was myself. I thought humans could learn about themselves through themselves, not through others. Wasn't it "I" who didn't go away from me from birth until death? Even asleep, I couldn't get away from myself. I had to live in conflict with myself all day, around the clock. It was painful. The more I had this feeling, the more I wanted to abuse myself. When I was furious, I didn't sleep for days on end. I fought sleep until my eyes hurt so much that I felt as if my eyeballs would pop out any minute, until my brain was submerged in a hazy fog, blurring everything in front of me. When I couldn't accept myself, I starved myself, separating the me who was hungry from the me who had no choice but to go hungry. I was content with watching the starving me and checked off hunger from the list of pain. That was when Uncle Hassan appeared in front of me.

Now I know how Aunt Anna must have felt the day she first met me, when I was stripped naked like the unembarrassed Belgian Little Man Pee. Uncle Hassan had asked her to give me a good bath. Outside her kitchen, through the back door, there was an outdoor faucet where she removed onion skins and outer layers of scallion, peeled potatoes, and gutted and scaled fish. I climbed into a huge round plastic tub filled with scalding water. Heat coursed through my body and soon the outermost layer of my skin looked bloated. Aunt Anna came out with a scrubbing pad gloved over her fingers and heaved a deep sigh at the sight of me. Then she gingerly stroked the scars all over my body.

She said that she had scars on her body too. I wasn't pleased with her assumption that she understood all about my pain, but I silently listened to her mutterings. A woman is bound to have scars after she's with a man or two, she said. Why, I asked, and she replied that men as a species couldn't live a single day without harassing women, and she looked daggers at me, though fleetingly, as if she'd realized that I, too, was male.

Aunt Anna was someone like a tin pot that heated up fast then turned cold as fast. That was why I grew disgruntled when people likened a person to earthenware as a compliment and to a tin pot as a putdown. People like a tin pot aren't necessarily worthless.

On my right arm, starting from where it bends, there is a scar that wraps down to my wrist, covering half of it, looking like an earthworm displaying its backside in a sandpit. Aunt Anna said this obviously was a burn from a boiling pot.

I don't know the origins of most of my scars. I do remember some. The scar on my left shin, according to the records, was from the third orphanage I was in. A heavy summer rain destroyed the foundation of the outhouse's cement-block wall, opening a three-meter-long gap as the fence collapsed in clumps along the cracks. The outside world, in full glory, swept in like a tsunami. Few kids remembered how long they'd been living in the orphanage. They'd been delivered to the place before anything could be registered in their brains. I learned the expression "delivered" from the truck driver who came every month with a load of relief goods. Unloading sacks of rice, flour, and sugar, he often muttered, "After I deliver these guys . . ." Somehow the term "these guys" sounded like he was referring to us.

I didn't remember anything, either. However hard I tried to remember the past, the stone-throwing of my memory didn't go over the orphanage fence. The orphanage was the whole world to me. Even if I'd experienced the pre-orphanage world, it was no more than a forgotten past, never to be teased out, unless placed under a hypnotic spell or something. Facing the collapsed fence after the rain, I shuddered at the sight of a strange world I'd never belonged in. What I saw was nothing special. Mundane. But it dawned on me that the world over the fence revealed itself to me, that the fence wasn't the cliff at the edge of our rectangular world. No kid was ready to venture out to the outside world through the wide opening, bigger than any door in the orphanage. I stepped up to the top of the collapsed blocks toward another world, defenseless now, the world in which there was no knowing what would be awaiting, the world that had been sectioned off and shut off with a single fence. A shriek came from behind. A large wobbling block fell toward me. That was how I hurt my shin. It was more excruciating for me that I'd failed to take even one step to the outside when a secret door opened than that I felt the smarting pain from the scrape.

When I first saw Uncle Hassan, I assumed I was being adopted abroad. Frankly, I was afraid. Walking behind him, I briefly entertained the thought of running away. By then, I wasn't stupid enough to venture out into the unfamiliar world without a penny in my pocket. It is possible that I didn't venture out through the gap of the collapsed fence because I knew too well that it would be pointless to join the outside world.

The stories tumbling out of the orphans who'd escaped but eventually been dragged back were similarly grim. Some of them fell prey to thugs who made money by selling the orphans' blood, while others encountered brutes who coerced them to beg on the street. None learned a useful trade. What they'd learned amounted to shining shoes, cleaning houses, and stealing, skills you could acquire on your own without any training.

The escapees claimed that their hardship was better than overseas adoption. They said that the adopted kids in foreign countries were required to donate their hearts, livers, or kidneys to the adoptive parents' birth children stricken with rare diseases. This sounded plausible. Why would they adopt orphans all the way from a small, poor country? Unless their plan was poaching, frying, or stewing them up to eat, that is. I'd have a nightmare that my inside was being hollowed out like a balloon, with my internal organs slipping out one at a time.

I thought Uncle Hassan's muscular arms would turn out to be a noose of fate that would stifle me some day. Later on, Uncle Hassan said, "Fate is a criminal known to the victim."

Ha! This kind of speech was ascribed to the popular television drama "Chief Investigator." Fate, living near us, hovers over us, desperately trying to shove us into a pit.

We let down our guard thinking we know it well, and fate, not missing a beat, finishes us off with its first and final kick. Uncle Hassan said, "So, Child, there's no fate that you haven't experienced. Oh bless this poor child. When you were born, you weren't the only one who was born. Your fate was born with you."

That day in the orphanage, fate succeeded in snatching me up. It was because I was caught off guard for a moment. Like the other kids, I should have scampered away to hide. But even after I spotted Uncle Hassan, I was standing there all alone, like a single wildflower in bloom on a vast open field, completely ignorant about what my fate would bring.

Where Uncle Hassan took me was different from where I'd stayed until then: orphanages, shelters, and a Catholic church. This was a rundown neighborhood on a hill, with alleys splitting and converging like a maze. We met no one on the way, which was quite extraordinary. It was a quiet afternoon. The sun was bright everywhere, but the paths we took were in the shade. Somewhere small children laughed. Soon, they appeared on the edge of the side road atop the steep stairs at the end of the alley we were walking along. The boys were all in T-shirts and shorts. They looked exactly the same; I wondered whether they were clones of one boy. The kids spat and jabbed an obscene gesture toward Uncle Hassan and disappeared in a flash, just as when they appeared.

I imagined their behavior was some usual mischief in the

neighborhood, an unwritten code of conduct circulating among children. The only thing that caught my attention was "Turkish bath!"—the taunt they'd thrown.

Uncle Hassan and I climbed the side road and took a break, huffing and puffing. Looking behind us, I noticed that the alley we'd taken was scarily steep. We could have taken the side road, but he'd opted for a shortcut. He took me to a cement-floored room furnished with a table and chairs that could be either Chinese or Japanese in style. His place was the first floor of a small two-story apartment.

Perched on a chair, I looked around. The rough-faced bare walls, without tiles or wallpaper, looked grim. Against one wall was a kitchen sink, and above it were two shelves neatly lined with bowls and dishes embossed with unfamiliar patterns. A coarse curtain covered a wood-latticed window opposite the entrance, and strands of sunlight seeped in through the curtain. The biggest difference I found about the room from any other place I'd been in was that the President's photo wasn't on display. Wherever I went, the same photo was hung where people would notice it first. I saw that here, at least, he wasn't a welcome figure.

A voice drifted in. A voice evoking an imagery of a gymnastic ribbon. Although it struck me as more desolate than a ribbon, it sounded as if yearning for something or resenting someone. When I turned my head this way and that to determine where it was coming from, Uncle Hassan said curtly, "A muezzin, calling to prayer."

He rolled out a prayer mat, which had been leaning against a corner. He took off his shoes and stepped on it. A pungent smell hit me. I wouldn't have found it funnier if a bear preformed what he did. Uncle Hassan bowed clumsily, slowly, doggedly as though he'd never done this before, just like a newborn puppy snuggling into its mother's breast. I'd briefly stayed at an orphanage run by the Buddhist Jogye Order, so I recognized his bows as similar to the Buddhists'.

Uncle Hassan said that this was the neighborhood and the house we were going to live in from then on. At least I wouldn't be tied down to an operating table in a foreign country to have my organs removed for donations. He shrugged, raked his thick moustache, and awkwardly waved at me, almost with an air of duty, before he went out. The scene would repeat itself every day from then on, but his back, reminding me of a hunched giant, exuded desperation and desolation, as if he were saying a final goodbye. His destination was less than fifty steps away, but every time he went there, he dragged his feet as if he were leaving his soul behind. Uncle Hassan was the first Muslim I had met, and as far as I knew, the only Muslim who butchered pork.

2

"He's stupid."

This was the orphanage director's reply when Uncle Hassan asked why I wasn't attending middle school. I felt insulted. If I'd had parents, they would have said, "He's smart but has a hard time focusing." True or not, parents are inclined to believe that.

Uncle Hassan wanted to send me to middle school. The admissions official at our neighborhood school flatly refused, saying that the admissions period was over.

He said, "His records show that he has a peculiar medical history. You've got to confirm it, but with that kind of illness, it will be difficult to find a school for him unless it's an alternative school."

Uncle Hassan asked around for alternative schools. Most were located too far, and a few that were close enough couldn't admit me right away. Sitting at the table, Uncle Hassan asked me, raking his wavy hair with his fingers, "This illness. Can you explain it?"

"I didn't want to go to school."

I'd been disgusted by everything they taught at school. The school mottos were mostly "cultivating upright citizens" and class mottos "sincerity, diligence, and cooperation." Whichever school it was, statues of stern historical figures sat in the flower garden and among them was always Yi Seungbok, the boy who attracted attention only one day a year for having been killed by North Korean guerrillas after screaming, "I hate commies!" Depending on the principal's preference, some schools had kitchen gardens where greens were grown and others had cages for pigeons or rabbits. In all schools, willows, roses of Sharon, evergreens, and junipers, all trimmed in the same style, stood without exuding much vitality, and a footpath was laid out around the playing field. Students were required to walk on a specific path set for them, and were trained to swear a pledge looking up at a piece of cloth covering the lectern on the podium. In short, school was where sincere fools were churned out. I was amazed at people who didn't abhor school. I couldn't understand, for the life of me, how they didn't find it horrifying that they were required to sit in the same posture in identical chairs at identical desks, nodding their heads together to unvaried lessons, or they spent their time laughing and crying, being beaten and scolded.

I explained these in a leering, smirking tone, as kids are apt to do these days. Uncle Hassan nodded. "So what did you do?"

"I chopped off the arm of the patriotic boy Yi Seungbok. I peed on the flower garden too."

"That wouldn't be enough for a diagnosis like this."

"I did it every day, at eleven o'clock sharp. Wherever I was, I dashed out at eleven. They didn't know what I was up to even when the trees in the flower garden wilted brown."

Uncle Hassan cocked his head. "I hope you're not doing that now. You don't have a choice for now, but you should go to school. If you're disgusted, go to school and retch there."

I didn't tell him that school was a lonely place. I didn't tell him that the gazes on me were detestable. I didn't tell him that I was fed up with the whispers and the dirty looks, the subtle mixture of sympathy and criticism.

The rundown apartment, where Uncle Hassan was renting, was so similar to other houses in the neighborhood that it was hard to tell them apart. All had a similar history. This was a product of the old age of the neighborhood. Just as cells divide themselves, houses bred. If there was the smallest empty space between two buildings, it was covered with tar-coated planks or tarps to pile up coal briquettes. As long as civil servants weren't meddlesome, residents encroached on public land to expand their properties. Even in the tiniest yard, people built a doghouse and an outhouse and stacked bricks to create an elevated flower garden.

The houses didn't only grow outward but ceaselessly expanded inward as well. People used a crawl space obtained by a lowered ceiling as an attic; they put up a ladder to climb into it and punched the wall to create a window to see the change of weather while lying down. If they had a gap big enough for spiders and moths to crawl or flutter about, they put in a board on which they slept or heaped their belongings.

Uncle Hassan's apartment was an example of failed attempts. The traces of his effort to renovate it in Turkish style let out a sad scream, overpowered by the Korean constraints. I don't mean that it was neither this nor that. This was a space like an alloy. Just as two completely different metals are dissolved into a new metal, this was a place with different temperaments and dispositions, a house I'd never imagined before.

The wall over the coal-briquette fireplace was scorched black, and a gridiron studded with sticky charred remnants hung on a rusty nail. This gridiron was used exclusively for kebabs. Every day a column of ants marched to the kitchen cabinet. Their destination was the sugar bowl. When the bowl was moved, the column slowly collapsed. It didn't take long, however, for the column—crawling across the wall from where the sugar bowl used to be, climbing along the edge of the two walls at an angle, and forming a horizontal line at the windowsill—to disappear into a crack in the window, like an animal swishing its long tail. When the lid of the sugar bowl was lifted, there were dead ants buried in an avalanche of sugar and some live ones climbing out of the bowl. If Uncle Hassan had a peerless skill, it was that he could randomly scoop up a spoon of sugar without a single ant in it. As far as I could tell, there might be some ants that spent their entire lifetime in that bowl.

The furniture and appliances absorbed the smells floating around the house in ordinary times but let them out in dank hours or on rainy days. Breathing in the odor that clung to me, I opened the narrow kitchen door to look down at the city. Outside the door was a protruding cement slab—the foundation of Uncle Hassan's apartment—which joined the lower neighbor's retaining wall. On the slab was a chair that perfectly fit my bottom, and Uncle Hassan perched on the chair at sundown, looked up at the dirty sky being dyed orange, down at the neighborhood where shabby crab-shell roofs sloped down, and at the inscrutable city. When I sat in the chair, I usually spat or threw garbage on the roofing shingles under my feet. I collected small stones to throw at tin sheets, including outhouse roofs, drain pipes, and gates missing a hinge or two. When a stone hit the tin, a light, unresonant thud slowly fanned out.

On rainy days, houses wept. Rainwater flowed in rivulets in every alley, and flimsy plastic umbrellas scurried to and fro. People trotted on, some in rainwear and rain boots and others under the umbrellas whose occasional protruding rib gave the impression of a bat wing. When Uncle Hassan was out, Uncle Amos came to visit. He told me about Athens, Sparta, Olympus, and Zeus and how azure the color of the Mediterranean was and how blue the Aegean Sea was. He told me how the wind from the Sahara changed after crossing the sea and how ships were anchored when a storm raged and waves rolled.

When Uncle Amos didn't come, I stripped to look at every inch of my body in a hand mirror. I thought I might recall a thing or two if I studied the scars whose origins I couldn't remember. I guess I was waiting for each scar to turn into a mouth and strike up a conversation with me. I couldn't even speculate how the deep dent under my right collarbone had come about. Aunt Anna, the queen of scars, couldn't offer any interpretation for that particular one. "You didn't get this gash from a whip or the blade of a shovel, for sure."

I had no doubt about that. I didn't want to believe that my parents abused me. I assumed all the marks had appeared after I was separated from my parents.

That was how I comforted myself every time. All the more so on rainy days. If not, the seemingly unceasing sound of rain might turn into Uranus's grip and snatch me up to take me somewhere else again. When I drifted off to sleep during the day, the institutions I'd stayed in floated up one by one. People who had mistreated me or discriminated against me made their appearance, too. No one I had liked appeared. This wasn't surprising, for I'd never liked anyone.

Even when I wasn't hungry, I boiled instant noodles. Making and slurping ramen alone, I savored anew that I wasn't in an orphanage. When I turned on the knob of the portable gas stove to raise the wick and ignited it with a match from the big matchbox with the brand name UN Match, dark smoke billowed out from the fuel hole. Jiggling the wick knob tamed the flames to a mellow blue. I loved the smell of burning gas. The burning of pure liquid, drilled from a distant desert or a stratified undersea rock, evoked the feeling of missing someone. According to Uncle Amos, soldiers on the battlefield believed that they were destined to go to paradise because the world they were enduring was hell. I couldn't accept that. Would a person whose life was hell be treated better in death? Could a person living in hell imagine a place that wasn't hell? All he could imagine would be another hell.

A long gaze at my scars made me dizzy as if I had astigmatism. When rain kept coming, I climbed the hill along the side road.

This was to see the turkeys and peacocks and pheasants that were kept in cages at a nearby school. On rainy days, piles of bird waste that had dried on the ground bubbled up, emitting a revolting smell, keeping other people away. Feeling on the nape of my neck the drops of water falling from the slate roof that precariously blocked the sky, I attempted a conversation with the birds, all my fingers hooked on the wire netting. *kut-kut-kut, pip-pip-pip, cluck-cluck-cluck, squawk-squawk-squawk, chirp-chirp- chirp, chachalaca, honk-honk-honk, gobble-gobble-gobble* . . . Birds, having flocked into a corner to avoid leaking holes on the roof, had no interest in talking to me, too busy rubbing against each other's forehead or beaks, puffing up their feathers, and shaking water off themselves. Baby birds with immature, twitching feathers kept their necks still and only pushed their heads back and forth as they went about aimlessly among grownup birds. They looked comical. There, I often came across a boy about my age. I recognized him as a boy who lived near Uncle Hassan's apartment.

One day, this boy threw an awkward smile my way when our eyes met. He used to look vacantly in my direction, holding a broom and a duster or a garbage bag. I couldn't tell whether his smile was sneering or sympathetic. The bridge of his nose was so low that his nostrils faced upward and his eyes were so narrow that it was impossible to tell whether they were open or shut. He looked like a baby gorilla. He waddled toward me, hunched over.

"Do you wan . . . want to, to know wha . . . what, these guys are saying?" He was pointing at the birds.

I wasn't surprised because I'd already known that he stammered, but it was frustrating to hear him out. With his eyes on me, his bluish lower lip trembled. No explanation was necessary about a boy who wandered about all alone on a rainy day like this. I nodded, although I wasn't curious about what the birds were saying. He beamed. Between his teeth, his short, red tongue, looking like a bird's, flickered in and out. Sounds came out when his tongue moved after a halt.

"They te . . . tell you to, to take . . . a hi . . . hike!"

I turned on my heels and walked away. As I climbed over the school's fence, the boy strained to keep up with me. I glared at him and he put on a vague smile.

"They te . . . tell me to, to take . . . a hi . . . hike, too!"

We waded in rainwater up to our ankles. Inside my sneakers my feet were bloated.

"I . . . I'm Yu . . . Yujong . . . Kim Yujong."

I nodded. I didn't ask but he added, "You know the no . . . novelist Kim Yujong. Right? He sta . . . stammered too. So I'll become a no . . . novelist."

Right. All one-eyed people are Captain Harok and all the long-haired are Matel in the animation Galaxy Express 999. *And any woman with a mole on her face is Marilyn Monroe. Stammering is an absolute requisite for becoming a novelist.* Regardless of his belief, if the novel is supposed to deal with the mistreated, the abused, and the stupid, Yujong and I could become the main characters of great novels, if not great novelists.

Before his family moved to this neighborhood, they'd lived near a zoo. He sneaked into the zoo through a hole in the fence every day and watched the animals. "You . . . you saw two, two dogs . . . stuck together, right? But I bet you did . . . didn't see ele . . . elephants do that."

Yujong had an ability to stimulate the imagination. He spewed out—of course haltingly—the habits and biological traits of all sorts of animals and insects that didn't inhabit Korean soil. When he said that he could fly on the back of a condor, an albatross, or a frigate bird, I imagined myself traveling the same way.

"I sneaked into the zoo for fi . . . five years. Some died or others were sent away when they got sick, and some were . . . were born or new . . . new ones arri . . . arrived."

The zoo occupants accepted Yujong as a regular, the same as their caretakers. Where Yujong lived was an illegal slum, and one day residents were driven away for having squatted on private property. The day before moving, Yujong hung around in the zoo the whole day. He said goodbye to all the familiar faces. It goes without saying that no animal waved goodbye to him.

"I . . . was sitting on the truck bed among bundles and look . . . looking up at the s . . . sky, and you know what? I heard them shouting . . . goodbye, Yu, Yujong . . . Bye. Be well and ha . . . happy."

That was when he realized that the silent world was constantly saying something. Yujong was not his real name. The zoo animals were the only ones he'd asked to call him Yujong. His mysterious ability to understand animal speech had been conceived a long time ago but was finally born at that moment on the moving truck.

I decided to believe this sweet tall tale of his. Believing is different from being deceived. Uncle Hassan said as much. "*La Ilaha Illallahu Muhamaadur Rasullulla*" (There is no one but Allah and Muhammad is his prophet). I asked him why he was deceived by such a lie, and he said that he believed it. He explained that when you believed a lie, it became a truth. I told him that I also believed: That my parents weren't bad people, that all my scars came from my bumbling mistakes.

Yujong and I became boys of the vast world. He was a chatty stammerer. To me at least. The longer we spent time together, the shorter our conversation grew. There was no need for him to stammer. He didn't stumble over words like Yeah, True, No, Humph, Bah. Just like a translation machine—although I don't know if such a thing exists—he changed animal languages into our language; to be precise, into the language handed down by our parents, the language he'd acquired where he used to live, the language used by the residents where we lived now. He translated their talk for me into a language mixed with various inflections and unknown vocabulary. This was far from amazing. The animal speech interpreted by Yujong was as deplorable as human speech. I must say that I was a little taken aback by the fact that animals threw out obscenities at the drop of a hat and that they lied left and right, just like people.

In any event, I talked with all the animals in the neighborhood through Yujong. It didn't do me any good. There was no hidden treasure where we lived. There wasn't any good-intentioned animal that revealed secrets hoarded from generation to generation, unlike in fairytales where the animals say things like human beings are "stupid fellows" and that "if you dig just a shovelful of dirt under you, you'll find gold and silver and treasures."

The only things they revealed were how pathetically and deplorably our neighbors acted. There were all sorts of people: Those who stole electricity from others, those who had sexual relations with their next-door neighbors, and those who didn't wipe their asses after taking a dump. It was no fun learning about these secrets. All sorts of trivial stuff were easily treated as secrets. Even secrets were shabby in the shabby neighborhood. No one had a fascinating secret about their parentage, but all had secrets about how they'd been conceived. There weren't any who stashed a lot of money away, but some hoarded a few pennies. There were people who concealed their true identities, but no disclosed identity would shock anyone. There were women disguised as men and men disguised as women, but no one was confused about their sex. Soon I lost interest. I found it tiring. Yujong had conversations with any animal, domestic or wild. I couldn't vouch that these domestic and wild animals understood what he said to them. He translated what they were saying, never asking them to do anything for us; there was no telling if they understood him. I asked him whether he could have a dialogue with any animal in the world.

"I didn't mee . . . meet all of them, but, but, probably, yeah . . . yes."

I asked which animal was the hardest to understand. "The sloth? The anteater? The platypus? The iguana? The armadillo? The Galapagos tortoise?"

Yujong stared at me and shot back, without even stammering, "People."

I didn't have the heart to ask, black, white, or yellow? He would have found it difficult to understand them, regardless of their skin color, sex, age, and nationality.

Actually, people had a hard time getting through to Yujong. He was often whipped by his teacher at school because he'd go to school with completely unrelated homework. At home, he was beaten because his parents had a hard time making him understand what they wanted from him. His sister would have beaten him up if she could. When he called out to her in the distance with the intention of giving her some candy, she ran away in the opposite direction. She was too pretty and cute to understand and love her stammering brother.

"Then how come you understand what I say?"

"You, you are not a person."

Looking at him leering after this wisecrack, I wished that I could put him in Noah's ark and send him up to the top of Mount Ararat and mete out the punishment of making him smile exactly like that for thousands of years. When he collapsed in exhaustion, let a condor swoop down and pick him up with its beak and fly to the Black Sea or the Mediterranean to drop him there with a big splash.

When it rained, I kept the front door open. Where did that water come from, pouring down so endlessly? I felt someone would enter at any minute, parting the beads of falling rain. It wasn't as if I were waiting for someone. I had no one in particular to wait for or long for. It was the sound of rainfall. It sounded as though someone were sticking half a matchstick into my ear. I was tickled as if I were on the verge of sneezing, but soon felt a piercing pain as if the clumsy hand touched some vital part in my ear. Whenever I felt this pain, I longed for someone for no reason. Real news might burst upon me from behind the rain, with the rain acting as the messenger. Although I didn't know what news it would be, my heart throbbed and my head ached. There couldn't be any good news coming to me, so I endured, all alone, the presumed sorrow, going beyond time, as if an inauspicious premonition had become a reality, as if a notification of death had arrived from the army.

In Uncle Hassan's pantry, gutter rats ran amok. They enjoyed the opportunity to gnaw at the tin sheets nailed down at the corners to block their entry. I couldn't understand as much as Yujong did, but I could tell what the rats were saying if I listened carefully. They were hungry. When it rained, many people went hungry. Yujong's parents, coal briquette sellers, were hungry, and so were the day laborers. I suffered from a different kind of hunger. The best way to forget it was reading. While reading sci-fi novels Yujong borrowed for me from his school library, I could forget everything.

Sweet was the future world unfolded in the stories. Human beings had the highest intellect and dominated the world. Robots took care of many things that used to be human chores. People didn't have to walk, even one step. They could live lying down their entire lives, if that was what they wanted, because they could teleport themselves. Yet, they were not always happy. They had to crack down on the robots' revolt and fight with superior invaders from other planets. When there was no invasion, people fought among themselves, stole from each other, and injured each other. The occasional war destroyed everything, forcing them to engage in a fierce competition for survival. Novelists imagined the future in their own ways. Sometimes they likened it to paradise, utopia, nirvana or *Gulistan* and at other times to hell, *Gehenna*, *Jahanum*, or *Muspelheim*.

When the rain kept falling even after I finished reading, I felt hollow. I felt as if I'd been instantly hurled back into the present from the future. A nagging question emerged. Why did novelists depict the future as a beautiful or an ugly place? Why didn't they think there might be no future? Just like the ants incarcerated in the sugar bowl, we might have been imprisoned on earth, wallowing in a sweet dream until the moment of our extinction. Why wasn't there a sci-fi fiction that depicted the world without human beings, the world consisting of sad, quiet deserts and wilderness?

I wanted to write a novel like that one day. A place where people didn't exist, an unimagined future for that very reason but had to be imagined at least once—I wanted to write about it before someone else did.

Uncle Amos said rain was a letter sent by a loved one. In his country, loved ones in distant places had the custom of staring at dark clouds. Then the clouds sent rain to where the beloved was, who gladly stood in the rain with their arms stretched out. Aunt Anna scoffed, commenting that if they did, their bodies would be covered with water warts and their heads would turn shiny bald.

When the rain died down, a drunkard appeared, as if out of nowhere. People called him the old locksmith. Defying his nickname, he didn't carry any key. He had a liquor bottle with him instead. His hands shook so much that he couldn't put his own key in his door. What he did have was a door that fit tightly to the doorframe. All he had to do was kick it open. He went home when it rained but when it cleared he was a fixture in front of the grocery, which was diagonally across from Aunt Anna's restaurant.

The day I arrived tailing Uncle Hassan, the locksmith was fixed on his spot. He looked twice as old as Uncle Hassan. His back was bent and he shuffled along, probably suffering from arthritis. His fingers, with bulging joints, shook like a typical drunkard's. Irregular furrows were etched deep on his brow even when he didn't frown. The day after my arrival, I sat, hugging my knees, in front of the locksmith, who was sitting cross-legged. Aunt Anna had earnestly told me that I shouldn't strike up a conversation with him. All he said was nonsense, she warned. "All day long he says pink elephants are passing by. Can anyone say he knows how to speak?"

I asked the locksmith, "Who am I?"

His stubby, dark-complexioned hands shook, almost touching the ground. "Elephant."

"What kind of elephant?"

"Pink elephant."

"What am I doing?"

"Passing by."

"Where am I headed?"

He didn't reply.

The first day I had spoken with Yujong, the locksmith made an appearance as usual soon after the weather cleared up. I put on slippers and rushed into the restaurant to pull AuntAnna to him.

"Who is she?"

"Elephant."

"What kind of elephant?"

"Pink elephant."

"What is she doing?"

"Passing by."

"Where is she headed?"

He didn't say anything.

Aunt Anna clucked her tongue, her eyes telling me, See? I protested. "But he knows how to speak!"

3

After Uncle Hassan went off to work at his butcher shop, I spent a good deal of time at Aunt Anna's. The gigantic signboard, Chungnam Restaurant, dwarfed her establishment, giving the impression that the building would collapse any minute, and I had to brace myself to step inside. But then, all the buildings in our neighborhood were like elderly people. Even newly built ones seemed to age overnight.

When she kept the kitchen's back door open, the pounding of her laundry paddle at the outside faucet drifted in. Also came the sound of splashing as she rinsed the laundry, pushing it into a big tub and then pulling it out, the sound of cascading water as she wrung it out, and the sound of shaking it out before putting it up on the clothesline. All these sounds were music to me. I believed music was all around us. Music was created by tapping, beating, plucking, or striking anything. Any noise giving pleasure to people could be music.

Her kitchen opened to the serving hall, with a cooking surface set against one solid wall and a low furnace below the window facing the street. Fitted to the opening atop the furnace, a big meat-boiling cauldron constantly set forth a cloud of steam.

Except for one side opening to the hall, all available wall spaces had built-in cupboards and sideboards from her eye-level to the ceiling.

The hall wasn't big, but she arranged tables so expertly that a good twenty people could sit down to eat and drink at the same time. The secret lay in narrow stools. She'd say, "People who don't have big rumps want to sit in big chairs. All they'll do is take off their shoes, sit cross-legged as if sitting on the floor, and scratch the soles of their feet. So why would I bring in big chairs?"

Practical Aunt Anna! She was also skilled at self-transformation. She'd changed the name of her restaurant to honor now this northern, now that southern province—Chungbuk Restaurant, Gangwon Restaurant, Jeju Restaurant, Jeolla Restaurant. She said her business had picked up after changing it to Chungnam Restaurant. So no one knew where she actually came from. Ditto with her real name. The book that left the deepest impression on her was Anna's Diary. Anne Frank writing Anna's diary? That sounded odd, but Aunt Anna claimed that she was sure Anna Frank, not Anne Frank, wrote the diary.

Much later in life, she confessed to me that she'd been confused about the title "Diary of Miss Anne"—some Korean editor must have added Miss to infuse an air of elegance with this formality—thinking it meant the "Diary of Miss Annae," a young bus conductress. When I asked her why she hadn't called herself Annae, she explained that she changed the ending slightly, afraid that Anne's fate of having been gassed to death would loom over her as well. Only then did I learn that Aunt Anna had been a teenage bus conductress. And that she'd never read *The Diary of Anne Frank*.

A rice cooker was installed near the outdoor faucet. This huge tin pot was harder to scrub down than an iron pot. Uncle Amos washed down the pot from time to time and because he did, he helped himself to a scoop of rice before it properly simmered down as if he were entitled to it.

I asked Aunt Anna, "Why are there so many people here who're not right in their heads?"

"Who do you mean? The old locksmith?"

"My next-door neighbor."

"Ah, the boy? Small as he is, he's a smart-aleck all right."

"Why? Is anything the matter with him?"

"Not as much as with you. You'll find out soon enough."

Yujong stood around in front of the restaurant. I walked to my house with him. As usual, Smart-aleck was sitting on a wide bench before his house. Crouched like a wounded animal, he gazed out at the world with unfocused eyes. At close range, his eyes were dark and round.

Pointing to him, Yujong told me that Smart-aleck had an incurable disease. When I asked him what it was, Yujong began to stammer a lot. This meant he didn't know. We circled him. We didn't know how to strike up a conversation with someone who had an incurable disease. Yujong cleared his throat but the boy must have thought we asked him a question. He started to give an answer to what we didn't ask.

"I was born in different places. Once I was born in a small village in France. I opened my eyes—I guess it was two days after my birth—and it couldn't have been worse. Wrapped in a dirty quilt that piglets could have frolicked on, I was laid in a cradle that squeaked horribly at the slightest movement because of its rusty nails and hinges. I wonder how many newborns greeted the world in that cursed cradle. It was dark all around. A weak sunlight managed to creep in from a tiny window and all sorts of insects were looking for a chance to bite me. Of course my parents were beautiful. But it was obvious that their beauty wouldn't last long. They already had wrinkles. So they died. After that, I was born and died in many different places. I didn't like any of them. But I had hope. Hope that I would be born as a prince or a princess." He sighed.

I decided it wasn't a good idea to give story books to sickly children.

"I sometimes lived fairly long. Like two months. I think it had to be two months because it was murderously hot when I was born, but the weather changed to a rainy season. I was born in a hamlet in India. I liked my silky skin. Next to my cradle were cows, sheep, and goats. In the shadow of a gigantic Banyan tree, I felt the cool breeze, I enjoyed the calm created by the sunlight refracted from the lake and the mood created by those rays. I didn't want to die. Like my father, I wanted to grow up to take a nap in a hammock and just like my grandfather, I wanted to age beautifully. But I contracted a disease that was beyond anyone's control. My parents took me to the city. I saw them for the last time in a dim hospital hallway. I died from a high fever just like a hot meteorite that had fallen from the sky."

Blood had drained from Smart-aleck's face as if he'd just died. Tears streamed down his cheeks. I tormented myself, wondering if I should keep listening to this nonsense.

Unaware of my internal turmoil, Smart-aleck gibbered on. "Ah, that was the greatest deception of all. When I opened my eyes, I found myself surrounded by gold curtains, and the sweet scent of thyme wafted into my nostrils. I heard a dignified, pleasant voice blessing my birth. Pale white clouds drifted in the blue sky, and jewels of all colors glittered before my eyes. They spooned sweet honeyed water into my mouth and clothed me in soft, warm velvet."

But the reality was that Smart-aleck was surrounded by faded old mosquito nets and the scent that stung his nostrils was the smell of mold thriving on the walls during the rainy season. Off the window by the head of Smart-aleck's bed was a public toilet, where almost thirty people of six households did their business as if waging a fierce battle. The stench drifting out of the toilet contributed to dulling Smart-aleck's power of reasoning.

Smart-aleck's father, afflicted with chronic asthma, wheezed with gurgling phlegm, and his mother, with no breasts to speak of, had fed him wheat bran porridge instead of her sweet breast milk, and when she didn't want to bother even with that, she fed him an inspired concoction of grain powder stirred into polluted water, sweetened with a sprinkle of saccharine.

Smart-aleck's parents had given birth to several children before they had him but lost them all. They didn't harbor any hope this time around. The malnourished child from his mother's womb was akin to a squashed frog flattened on the road. They neglected their child, believing that his fate had been determined regardless of their effort.

"When I realized that I had been deceived, I made up my mind to die, just as I did in my previous life. I didn't have to make any effort, because it was an easy thing to do. How long could a baby survive in an unsanitary room, swaddled in a damp blanket infused with all sorts of human secretions and dirty words from hopeless gamblers? The stable where Jesus was born couldn't compete with my room in terms of hopelessness. If Jesus had seen me, he couldn't have conceived the idea of serving the lowliest of the low. When I got tired of sucking my mother's empty breasts, grimy with dirt, I bawled, entreating that I be taken out of this world as soon as possible. When I fell asleep, I had a nightmare—it was about me surviving it all and then suffering all my life as the head of a household carrying the family's fate on my shoulders and aging and dying ever so slowly. What nightmare can be more terrible than that? God is mean-spirited. He ignores people who don't want to die and dumps people who want to live on a jet plane heading for hell."

He pointed up at one side of the sky. No jet plane was in sight. There was only a disappearing ribbon of trails from a plane.

"A few days ago, the rice shop's second daughter vanished like smoke. Fate took that loose girl, as if a kite flew down and snatched up a chick. If you really want to disappear from this world without a peep, you should regard the world as a place worth living in and you should have a strong desire to live. But I don't have any desire. That's why I can't die. It's so unfair. I didn't want to get born, but someone kicked my ass and pushed me into this world. Who did that?"

Tricked by his parents' scheme to bind him to this world, he had no choice but to linger on earth. The world where he belonged was not here but somewhere else, so this world was merely a foster home for him. All he did as he stayed in his foster world was to sit in front of his house, glaring at passersby, or luring cats and dogs so he could harass them. A yellow- striped cat, her emaciated belly almost touching the ground, skulked by.

"Even cats ignore me. No wonder I don't want to live. I can't believe that in order to die, you must first have a desire to live."

He didn't care what reactions we showed to his talk. In a word, he acted like an apostrophe. He inserted or removed himself between Yujong and me as he saw fit. When he was involved, a cacophony occurred without fail. When I told him about Yujong's special ability, he put on an insulted look.

"Hah! Did you think I'd swallow that? Then tell me what this cat is saying."

The yellow-striped cat passed by again, pretending to be scared of us but oddly offending us as we carefully watched her.

Yujong stammered, "Stu . . . stupid bo . . . boys."

It was expected. What else could that cat say? A short, ugly fellow living with a Muslim who cleaved off meat from pig carcasses, a stammering boy who claimed to understand animal language, and a jabbering kid who could mutter complaints all day long if he was given half a chance. Regarding the trio, anyone would have said the same thing. Smart-aleck laughed so hard that his jaws almost came apart. I'd never seen anyone laughing with a blank expression like him. Yujong shrugged, as if he couldn't help it.

"You . . . you like the second dau . . . daughter of the rice shop, right? People saw . . . saw you whim . . . pering the day she dis . . . disappeared."

Smart-aleck shuddered like a frog that was caught by its hind legs and thrown to the ground. I thought, Hey, what's there to be so worked up over a thing like that, you gibbering kid? He could have fainted if we'd told him all the secrets we knew about our neighbors.

Uncle Hassan said that poverty and love were like sharp nails in your pocket. You could ignore them but they would poke through sooner or later. If they didn't push themselves outward, the nails would have already pierced into the flesh of the pocket's owner like the hook of a harpoon.

Smart-aleck's excitement didn't last long. That seemed to be his disposition. We saw him luring the yellow-striped cat with a poisoned dead rat as bait. We expected that a vendetta would ensue, but he unexpectedly tickled the cat under her chin with his thin finger. The cat rubbed her face and belly against his knee. The boy was getting acquainted with an assistant who'd eventually share his secret. How earnestly he must have been yearning for the exposure of his secret!

The next day, I went to the park with Uncle Hassan. Like other Muslims, he took the day off on Friday.

On other days, he finished his first prayer of the day at sunrise and went to work in his cotton pants and sheepskin shoes. Entering his shop, he took his work clothes out of the closet and changed into them. Then, he wiped the scale and the chopping block and sharpened his knives, splashing water over the whetstone from time to time. For a while, the gray water flowing over the whetstone gurgled down the drain on the floor. Finally, when the shiny knives refracted sunlight into his eyes, they were ready to handle the meat. After he took out lumps of meat from the freezer, he took a short break, waiting for the meat to thaw slightly for easier knife work.

This was when he drank a cup of coffee. Squatting in front of his shop, he enjoyed the most serene moments of his day. In these moments at least, his gaze, absently directed to passersby, sparkled like a dew-covered wildflower. He described his coffee as being dark as hell, strong as death, and sweet as love.

After finishing his coffee, he drank water to rinse out his mouth and put on cotton gloves he'd washed and hung out to dry the day before. Carefully prodding the meat with his gloved hands, he checked whether it had thawed to his liking. Laid out on one side of the chopping block was a pair of knives: a thin, sharp-pointed cleaver to separate bones, and a fat-bellied knife resembling a mackerel. His hands had an intricate web of thin white lines: healed knife scars. Even after a careful examination, it wasn't easy for him to separate bones embedded in the flesh. The knife slid when it encountered unexpected bones, but he didn't get hurt easily. The scars on his hands were from long ago. Now he knew how to control his grip to prevent being cut when his knife slipped. He'd acquired this skill over the years. Before customers arrived, he sliced pork belly and cut out meat for soup, the most demanded parts. The rest he cut out or sliced in their presence.

Once, a customer asked him why he wasn't using a machine, pointing to his scars. Like any seasoned Korean butcher, he answered with a smile, "Hand-cut meat tastes better." By the end of a day, he had a few handfuls of leftover scraps. They were handed over to Aunt Anna to be transformed into sausage soup on her customers' tables.

Uncle Hassan spoke little all day long. All he did was cut up a portion upon a customer's request and wrap it up in newspapers before putting it in a plastic bag. Few words were exchanged. None of his Korean customers had any interest in the Muslim, who was clad in blood-splattered clothes and cutting up pork with a big knife. Even if they had, I doubt that they could have shown it, intimidated as they were by his grave demeanor.

When he came home after work, he rested, perching on a chair and resting his feet on the table. He'd fall asleep, curled up in a curious shape, just like a freshly toasted dried fish. He exuded an eerie air, as he made no sound in his sleep; he looked dead.

I studied his scarred hands while he dozed. The origins of his scars were obvious. The longer I looked at them, however, the more I felt that the origins didn't matter. I don't like sentimental comments, such as a scarred person recognizes another scarred person. Still, I couldn't help feeling moved. The knife marks etched on his old dry skin gave me the illusion that his fortune-telling palm lines escaped their home to crisscross his entire hand. At times, I gingerly touched his squashed ears that had lost their original shape. If a tormented face were to be cut out for a scrapbook, it would give me the same feeling, I thought. Late some nights, a proselytizer from a pioneering church made a visit. Most neighbors were too poor to attend a service and even when they did at the proselytizers' urging, they soon lost interest and stopped going. This new proselytizer was persistent. He considered it his mission to rescue Uncle Hassan from hellfire. After my arrival, he had another Satan to save. The word "proselytizer" implied that he had another mission in addition to the simple conversion of faith: the triumph of Christianity over Islam.

Before reaching our home, he had to patiently listen to Smart-aleck's nattering. He seemed to regard this as an inevitable sacrifice he had to make. Only when Smart-aleck started ignoring him and muttering to himself, did he clear his throat and knock on our door.

Uncle Hassan opened his eyes a crack to wonder briefly what had awoken him. Then he roused himself in the reverse order of when he fell asleep and opened the door. The proselytizer adjusted his clothing to make sure that his attire was in good order and tried his best to take on a stern expression just like Moses' at the time of upholding the Archangel's order. At times, a dirty smile spread around his mouth as if he were a crusader excited about the prospects of conquest and plundering, and at other times a sly, blasphemous smile danced around his lips as if he were a Freemason going out to a holy war.

Uncle Hassan was not pleased to see anyone at his door, but he didn't send anyone off, either. He didn't shut the door in anyone's face—be it a tonsured Buddhist monk, an itinerant fortune-teller, a pastor, or a priest—although he didn't welcome them wholeheartedly. In the same vein, he let them say what they wanted to, sitting across from them. None, however, succeeded in drawing out a flicker of interest, let alone admiration, from him. Actually, I wondered if he listened to them at all. Then even the religious people, whose patience is considered to be relatively infinite by themselves and those around them, would be discouraged of their own accord and grow pessimistic. When they left, all of them looked distraught, as if they'd been forced to kiss a demon, and they were displeased as if they'd glimpsed secrets lurking in human life. The proselytizer in question was different, however. He didn't get tired; he came and went diligently. He stole miscellaneous items from us, though, which is the typical behavior of people who feel they are unfairly treated.

Uncle Hassan promised that he'd take me to the park on his day off. Friday came around, the holiday for all the Muslims in the world. I wasn't particularly happy to go for a walk at the park. It was hard to get used to harsh gazes and whispers. I'd known for a long time that misfortune and tragedy could be the objects of sympathy when they belonged to someone else entirely. We generally don't like people who are like us. What we confirm through those who are like us—the poor, the oppressed, and the neglected—is that human beings are boundlessly weak, and that we are not so different from those dirty, terrible people.

People were afraid of Uncle Hassan, although he'd never frightened or mistreated them, nor did he carry a hidden weapon. They were afraid of him for a single reason: he was different from them. Because he had a moustache, because his eyes were deeper set and darker.

I'm sure the one who enunciated the idea that differences were only shadows of similarities must have led a happy life. No one would argue against the fact that difference is a shadow of similarity. The one who proclaimed this quip had to be a happy person because he didn't take into consideration the fact that even if you know this, you can't do anything about your emerging displeasure and fear, the natural fact that aversion to others is bound to continue until the cause of the feeling is removed or until a good reason to justify the disgust can be found, just as it is difficult to stop the flow of urine once you start until your bladder empties.

Some weren't afraid of Uncle Hassan. Toddlers, swaddled babies who had just opened their eyes to the world, and the fetuses curled in their mothers' wombs—those who hadn't been taught that it was okay to look down on others because of their differences burst into merry laughter at the sight of him. Toddlers approached him and clutched his pant leg. Their parents, faces blanched like the parents in a legend who had to put their only daughter at the mercy of a boa constrictor, were at a loss for what to do, whether they should fight the monster or let the monster do as he pleased, hoping that he would show benevolence and generosity. Uncle Hassan squatted in front of the child, revealed his yellow teeth, twisted up the tips of his moustache, or put on his eyebrow magic show, the show that never failed to throw Aunt Anna into a fit of laughter. Still, the parents didn't let their guard down.

Uncle Hassan would let the child pull his moustache or lift his hat and throw it down to the ground, gently stroking the child's head with his forefinger.

Our stroll through the park continued. In the park, there were many people who were especially afraid of Uncle Hassan. Most of them transported miscellaneous goods, groceries, and electronic goods smuggled out of the American military base; hustled customers to bars; or wasted their energy chasing women. When Uncle Hassan came into view, they stuck cigarettes in the corners of their mouths to strike a tough-guy pose. If Uncle Hassan lifted his head to glance at them, they avoided his gaze. If he took a step toward them, they scattered like a horde of cockroaches, hiding behind the shield of plane trees or fleeing into the public toilet. Once we entered the toilet to take a leak and came across a foolish sacrificial lamb who had been waiting for the monster to pass through. He was a dark-complexioned young man with thick lips and slightly curly hair. His dark, dilated eyeballs rolled, like those of a mouse chased by a cat to a dead end. He must have thought he had found a helper in me; he threw me a meaningful glance, signaling for help. I knew that nothing would happen, but I mischievously put up my hands to my neck and pretended to strangle myself. Seized with despair, the curly-haired man, his shoulders hunched, carefully watched Uncle Hassan as he went up to a urinal, pulled down his zipper, and peed. I bet the toilet had never been cleaned from the day of its opening; it was disgustingly filthy. A sour, revolting stench from the rotting human waste stung my nose. I felt as if I were standing in front of hell, my nose stuck to the cracks of its door. The young man looked pitiful, like a member of Maruta, the Japanese Imperial Army's human experiment subjects, standing in a gas chamber. He was on the verge of tears, and then ready to faint. He was bracing himself in desperation with a diminishing sense of pride. He knew that he'd soil his clothes if he allowed himself to faint there. He seemed to regard Uncle Hassan as a serial killer on the loose or something.

Our short walk through the park satisfied Uncle Hassan. Throughout our stroll, his gaze lingered on every object in the park: from the bare earth strewn with stones to the sky where clouds, like a patchwork quilt, were afloat; from the fractured sunlight under our feet to the tops of well-groomed trees; from woodlice inhabiting dark, dank corners to squirrels scampering from tree to tree. He strolled leisurely as if he were ambling through a garden attached to a grand house with an old friend.

I had no idea what his home country was like. I was in the dark about the village of his birth and about his childhood. Did pines and oaks thrive there, too? Did sparrows, doves, and magpies fly in the sky? Did long-horned beetles and earwigs live on tree stumps? What color was the sky and what smell did the wind carry? I could only guess. I also knew that I'd feel at home there, even if trees I'd never seen formed a forest and strange animals dwelled there.

I didn't have a hometown, anyway. I didn't have a memory of an archetypical landscape to long for or familiar objects to make me dream of returning. So wherever I went, it'd be my hometown and my home country. Whomever I met could be a longtime friend or my family. It also meant that no place was my hometown and no one was my friend or family.

The voice of a muezzin came from afar. Uncle Hassan looked down. The mosque held a prayer gathering every Friday, and Muslims congregated there. Uncle Hassan didn't attend it. I had no idea when he'd stopped going.

4

We would come across the occasional person heading for the mosque. One of them was the imam, the cleric. He didn't strike me as anyone special despite his duty of carrying out God's command on a daily basis. His old suit pants completely covered his shoes but every time he bent his knees, the scrubby tips of his shoes came into view. His T-shirt was so faded that its original color was indeterminable. He'd easily blend into any group of old Korean men as far as I could tell.

The imam was transformed only when he was leading prayers at the mosque. I'd seen him decked out in formal wear. The white robe he donned was useful in many ways. Wearing it, he was set apart from other Muslims who'd gathered to worship. The robe concealed his cheap clothes. The imam's cap in the shape of a Japanese dumpling was useful as well. It covered up his disheveled hair, and he looked neat after tucking stray hair under it. Whenever he bowed, his red, squashed-looking cap looked like a gigantic tongue darting in and out of a mouth.

Uncle Hassan didn't acknowledge the imam on the street; he ignored him. This description isn't quite right. Let me put it this way: When his eyes met the imam's, Uncle Hassan looked through him. To Uncle Hassan, the cleric was no different from an invisible man. The imam, on the other hand, didn't have the knack of treating Uncle Hassan as invisible. All he could do was freeze up, as most foreigners in our neighborhood were inclined to do. I had a conversation with the cleric because he initiated it. He had a thick voice, divorced of holiness or dignity. It was the voice of a poor, timid foreigner. I thought the imam had something to do with Uncle Hassan's refusal to go to the mosque on Fridays despite his observance of the day as a Muslim. I guessed it by the way Uncle Hassan said to me, "He's a ghost. You shouldn't look at him. Even if you do, don't show that you did." The imam looked twice as old as Uncle Hassan. His hands, with bulging joints, shook like an alcoholic's, and irregular furrows ran deeply on his brow even when he didn't scowl. Aunt Anna referred to him as "a living ghost."

If he had been a ghost, his shadow could have been his real body. Actually, he flinched when someone stepped on his shadow. For some reason, his shadow looked more human to me.

I'd known a person just like that. I don't remember how many orphanages I'd lived in before the particular one I'm talking about. This orphanage was a single-story building at the foot of a mountain. Either the orphanage was attached to a Catholic church or the other way around. The church, looking down over a small city, was reminiscent of the mount where Jesus gave his famous sermon. The priest there strived to be a model of hope. Whether the son of God or prophets, all promised a rosy future. Even the head of our shabby neighborhood had a list of futile hopes for our area: the improvement of the narrow, dilapidated roads and an abundant flow of water from every faucet.

The priest was different from them in that he made efforts to make such hopes come true. He was partially successful. But his success was brief, and memories of him faded like a grandson's recollection of his grandfather.

The priest was mute. He didn't stammer like Yujong, but he'd lost his hearing in a childhood accident at a mine and couldn't speak from then on. It was rumored that his father had been trapped in an underground shaft and the boy was anxiously calling his father down the dizzyingly distant shaft until his uvula fell off. Whatever the truth, I didn't doubt that he was from a mining village.

He worked like a miner. He donned work clothes more often than priest's garb. He tended the flower bed, grew vegetables in the kitchen garden, laid foundations and built outhouses and such, and maintained or repaired them. Mischievous kids got a rap with his thick, callused palm. He couldn't speak or didn't speak, so we liked this young priest much more than the other priest, who was much older.

When he took a break from his labor, I stepped into his shadow. The warm and sweaty smell wafting from him was sweet. The shadow he made was small, but enough to embrace me. Staying there, I felt I was being taken care of within a sturdy fence. When he looked at me, his eyes were as gentle as Mary's in the fresco at the church entrance. Mother of all men. The priest was male, but I sensed motherly love from him. I believed I could find soft, buxom breasts if only I touched his chest. I didn't have the ability to understand what a mute person was conveying. I didn't see him use sign language, either.

But I could guess what he silently conveyed, and I thought he understood what I told him. So I remember what he conveyed to me. He pointed at his muscular arm with his finger. His blue-veined wrist was tough and sturdy like an old oak.

"Child, your face, your body, is not proof of your soul, just as red blood is drawn from this blue vein."

This was how he comforted my soul. Several days after this conversation, he was looking down at the small town, where his congregation was engaged in arduous daily lives. Behind him was a truck that had just delivered building materials. The truck's parking brake failed and it went over the stones propped against its back wheels and slid down, hitting the priest who had no inkling of what was happening. His firm back was broken and his muscular thighs and forearms were crushed. Vivid red blood, seemingly shielded from the sunlight until then, gurgled out of his mouth and wounds, soaking the porous, light brown dirt in the front yard of his beloved church.

He went to permanent sleep, with his calm eyes open, reflecting the sky. His rosary beads, scattered with a snap of string, rolled down toward the town.

Had he known what his fate would be like? Had he known that he would be born as a poor miner's son, that he'd grow up longing for his mother, the woman who ran away from poverty, that he'd lose his voice and his father, that an old priest and a nun would take him in, that he'd wear a priest's garb, and that he'd die with a cracked head and a broken back while doing repair work at an orphanage? If he'd known it, would he have still wanted to be born?

The priest who looked like Mary, my mother, was gone like that. The church remained but the orphanage was shut down. Once again, we scattered all over through the narrow channel open to us. The blue vein was the prison of red blood. I told a lot of people about the priest's death.

After my recounting, Uncle Hassan said, "God bless him!" and Aunt Anna said that the priest could have been her own son, for all she knew. Uncle Amos started saying, "Oh, holy Christian. With your flesh and blood, you tried to make this godless, cursed place the blessed land, and . . ." but was cut off by Aunt Anna's sharp reproach, as usual.

As for me, I had nothing to say. Even if the priest was resurrected like Jesus, I wouldn't welcome him if his shadow didn't come back with him. He taught me at the final moment of his life that a person is one and the same with his shadow. When he collapsed, when he gasped and doubled over in the front yard of the church, with his head, elbows, and knees touching the ground as if in supplication, his shadow was precisely folded and tucked into his body, became part of his soul, and vanished altogether. Death means the disappearance of one's shadow. God seems to take back a person's life, but in reality He allows a human being to gather back his own shadow. Aided by the warmth of the priest's temperature, by the moisture from his body, red blood left a fresco where its owner had lain, in place of where his shadow used to be—his final shadow, the trace of his journey in this world. In the same way as Mary's image had been drawn at the church entrance.

I didn't feel any pain when I stood in the priest's shadow. An inexplicable sorrow would vanish as if the scars on my body had disappeared, as if the dents had been filled up, as if a new layer of skin had grown taut and drawn into the rest of my skin, as if goose bumps had died down unnoticeably. Even if some had tried to hurt me, they couldn't have had their way at that moment. The priest's shadow was big enough to cover the earth with still some left over. Covering scars is a great feat indeed.

I didn't know that the truck was sliding down. No one knew. I shouted. The young priest looked in my direction and raised his arm. Just like an extra in a war movie. Soon after the accident, the priest raised his head again to look down at the town and I probably followed suit. When the truck hit the priest and crushed him before getting stuck in the gutter on the edge of the slope, shafts of sunlight peeked out of clouds, shining down on the town. The sky seemed to be throwing bunches of silver arrows to the earth.

The truth of the matter is, however, we couldn't overcome the barrier of the old priest. So, my memory is fiction. I didn't know how the mute priest died, and I couldn't accept his death for real. I simply intuited that I'd no longer be able to enter his mysterious shadow.

I witnessed the splendid tragedy in my imagination. Only the shadow was vivid in the haphazard collage I'd put together from the fragments lifted from the images I'd seen, from war movies, television dramas, and cartoons. I don't agree that shadows are dark, black, or gray. The shadow adds vividness to the object that casts it. It turns brown dirt more brown, red bricks redder, blue water bluer: The shadows allow all objects—to which we haven't paid attention under the glaring sun—to regain their inherent colors. The shadow gives breathing room to all things on earth, the things that cannot avoid the sunlight, and by concealing itself, the shadow actually reveals itself. If you're at your wit's end, just like someone looking for a perfect hiding place that no one would check, the shadow will be your final haven. Because something is bound to be there, having crept into it looking for a place to hide.

That was the last image of the priest in my memory. The unchanging mundane life was what the priest kept his eyes on, the priest who beamed without making a sound, as if guiding and welcoming the poverty-stricken congregation climbing the steep hill to attend Mass he would preside over. We prayed, sitting around the old priest, as if safeguarding him. His voice reminded me of a feeble animal that had gone through thorn bushes. The church bell rang far into the distance and it suddenly occurred to me that the sound, once departed, would never return to its original place. I shed a tear.

I knew that one day in the future, though I couldn't tell when it would be, I'd completely forget about this church, the orphanage, and the mute priest, and I knew that even when I recalled, from time to time, this very moment, which would be in the past then, it would be remembered as vague impressions and feelings, not as a clear, concrete object. If the sound of the bell dispersed in the air, it would be still flying somewhere in the universe. Until it reached God, the ringing would ceaselessly wander about in the dark, vast universe just like the Wandering Jew.

I took special care not to step onto the imam's shadow. To do so, I always had to make sure that he'd face the sun. When the sunlight was slowly lowering itself toward the horizon like a person laying his tired body down, the imam shaded his eyes with his hands. The imam's pale face, dyed orange, looked like well-baked bread; I imagined how delicious it would be if I bit into his cheek.

Uncle Hassan threw a glance at the mosque on his way back home. I stopped by at Aunt Anna's eatery and recounted what had happened at the park. She was prone to tears. She regretted anything that she hadn't been part of.

I spotted the rice shop's second daughter trudging behind her father, a Kim, along the side road. I squatted in front of the locksmith, the drunkard. The girl had a flat face and her ponytail swayed to and fro like a pendulum with every step she took. Her face looked like a small *chonggak* kimchi that was bitten into, with the white root almost gone from a big bite and the strands of leaves left intact. The side road was a path where life was loaded and delivered, I thought.

I asked the locksmith. "Who is she?"

"Elephant."

"What kind of elephant?"

"Pink elephant."

"What is she doing?"

"Passing by."

"Where is she headed?"

He didn't say anything.

The girl passed, alternating her gaze between me and the drunkard. Her eyes said: What did I expect other than seeing those tiresome guys again! I threw her the same gaze.

5

Uncle Amos broke out in hives if he didn't lie.

One day I found him covered with a rash from food poisoning; he'd eaten spoiled food at the hospital where he worked. I knew that he was sick by the way his feet, poking out of his window, were in spasms. Pale, he wiped cold sweat off his forehead with the back of an equally pallid hand.

He mumbled, "The damn devils put poison in my food. They were mad at me because I didn't lie for several days. Looking back, I've been too good recently. I'm too sick to tell lies now and look how I'm getting worse! Once you stop lying, that's the end of you."

He bit down on his lip hard, leaving teeth marks, as if he'd regretted mightily that he'd carried himself good and meek for the past few days. Up to that point, only Yujong and I believed Uncle Amos' lies more than twice.

Uncle Amos couldn't eat anything. He threw up as soon as he swallowed anything. Seized with a high fever, he complained that he saw only darkness before his eyes. Aunt Anna, muttering, laid a damp towel on his wrinkled brow.

Soon his fever subsided under the influence of her curative powers. He pretended he was still sick, however, gibbering nonsense. He managed to hold onto her thick wrist with his trembling pallid hand as he jabbered, his eyes glistening with some odd fever. "Oh, you beautiful woman! You're my Aphrodite. You're more dazzling than white marble from Mount Pentelicon. You're truly my goddess. If you want, I can stand in the middle of an Athens plaza and loudly confess what's in my heart to reach the One residing in heaven even if idiotic men become jealous of me and blind folks mock or look down on me."

He dramatically let go of her wrist and slowly turned his head sideways, shutting his eyes. He didn't forget to drop a tear from his closed eyelid. He fell asleep peacefully, like someone who'd fulfilled his duty. Aunt Anna decided to be duped again, just this once. She straightened out his bedding by rolling his sleeping body, heavy as a corpse, this way and that; cleaned every nook and cranny of his narrow attic room; placed a pitcher full of barley tea and a bowl near his bed, and ran her thick, nimble fingers through his disheveled salt-and-pepper hair for a combed look, as if prodding pork to examine its quality.

Standing in front of the eatery, I could guess what was going on in the room above by the way his feet went in and out of the window and rolled this way and that. When Aunt Anna went down to her restaurant, his feet disappeared and his head popped out instead. He was ready to throw taunts at passersby or spit on them, as usual. At times his mouth squirmed just like a goldfish on the surface of water, opening and closing its mouth to breathe.

Uncle Amos had a welt as wide as a pinky on the left side of his chin. I was instinctively attuned to scars. I believed that all scars had mutual relations, just like languages, regardless of their origins, whether they were congenital or created by violence or mistake. Uncle Amos claimed that the mark was where his gill used to be. As a boy, he could dive into the Aegean Sea and cross it without having to pop up, even once, just like a submarine. When he joined the army, this ability was recognized, resulting in his transfer to a special unit. One day during a military operation, he came across a mermaid. He was dragged to her golden underwater palace, where he was treated with courtesy fit for a sultan. He spent only a day there, but in the real world an entire year had passed. I asked him why he'd escaped the golden palace, and he tapped his chest and said, "I was an honorable soldier."

He was treated as a defector and incarcerated in a brig, a renovated former fortress of the Temple Cavalry, located on an island in the middle of the vast sea, where not even a passing ship came into sight. He escaped the prison by jumping off a cliff hundreds of feet high. I asked him what happened to his gill and he thought it over for a while before he answered, "The mermaid was afraid that I'd run away, so she soldered it shut. Her eyes were swollen because she suffered from a chronic stomach ailment. You should have seen her, her eyes popped out just like a frog's. That was so funny."

Uncle Amos was funny.

There were many funny people, actually. Yujong's homeroom teacher gave a confusing talk during a morning roll call. He told his students a story that was dear to him. It was about a top student and a worst student. He said that the first place was meaningful only when there was a second best and a third best. There would be no top student without the worst scorer. At this point, the teacher's eyes met Yujong's. The students took his lecture differently from what he'd intended. His long-winded speech threw half-awake children into more of a haze. They wondered if they were meaningless beings whose sole purpose of existence was to glorify the top student. No explanation was offered to correct their interpretation, so most of them didn't have their doubts dispelled; they accepted what they understood as truth. Yujong was literally the worst student in class. It goes without saying that he grew despondent. Even before Yujong finished telling us this story, Uncle Amos got agitated. Everyone is equal before God, he cried. This wasn't credible to us. Uncle Amos was living proof that everyone wasn't equal before God.

Uncle Amos promised that he'd take revenge for Yujong. Then he went around babbling about his pledge to anyone who was willing to listen.

The next day, we were at Aunt Anna's after late lunch. Uncle Hassan, Uncle Amos, Aunt Anna, and I were sitting around drinking Aunt Anna's notorious instant coffee when we noticed Yujong's homeroom teacher marching down the slope. Yujong was trailing him. The teacher stopped at the restaurant, looked back at Yujong, and asked whether this was the right place. He then strode in. His eyes landed on Uncle Hassan and then Uncle Amos. The teacher looked uneasy, most probably because of Uncle Hassan. He didn't know to whom he should take his case, so he asked Yujong who was the right one. The boy pointed to Uncle Amos. The teacher instantly recovered his color. He pulled a chair up next to Uncle Amos and as he was lowering himself, he slipped and thumped his bottom on the floor. This happened often at Aunt Anna's. He complained about the smallness of the chair but when no one responded, he carefully tapped the table with his palm as he would rap his lectern during a lesson. Still no one paid attention. Uncle Hassan went off to his butcher shop and Aunt Anna slipped into her kitchen. I sat in a corner and cut out newspapers for my scrapbook. I cut out only people's faces. Outside the restaurant, Yujong started talking to the yellow-striped cat.

The teacher asked, "Are you the one who vowed to take revenge on me?"

Uncle Amos didn't say anything. Silence for a stretch of time.

"Do you speak Korean?"

Uncle Amos shook his head. The teacher nodded as if he understood now. No encounter could have been more idiotic. The teacher addressed Aunt Anna: "People call something like this an incident, you know," and then he left. Uncle Amos wouldn't have flinched even if the President had come to visit. The teacher's visit was nothing to him.

The neighborhood residents' volunteer firefighting squad carried out a monthly campaign to alert people to the dangers of fire. During the most recent campaign, Uncle Amos carried around a red-painted iron hook and shouted, "Fire! Fire!" Real fire trucks rushed over and the fire station chief, in leather boots, kicked the captain of the volunteer firefighting squad for having raised false alarms. Uncle Amos had done this mischief while the other volunteers were sleeping. He shut himself off in his room with his window closed and didn't come out for days.

Aunt Anna said to me, "I smell a crazy volunteer firefighter's corpse rotting up there. Go check. See if he's alive or dead. If he's dead, let's throw him in the Han River. So he'll float all the way to the Aegean Sea or whatever. If he's still alive, tell him to scurry down. Otherwise, I'll throw him in the boiling pot." Uncle Amos, having closed the window opening to the street, kept the opposite window open. With his feet poking out that hole, he was reading. He winked at me. "Don't worry. I don't have to work as a laundry orderly anymore. I have lots of good Korean friends."

He had been fired from the general hospital's laundry. In the past, he'd followed his good Korean friends to the countryside. It goes without saying that he returned a beggar. He'd been stripped clean, wallet and clothes, by his good Korean friends. He said, "The devil was an angel in the beginning. I'll teach Satan a lesson for driving my good friends to hell."

Up in his attic, I relayed Aunt Anna's words verbatim. Uncle Amos said that he was fine, that he wasn't that hungry. Going for a week without food had been no big deal during the war, he said. He claimed that once he hadn't eaten anything for as long as two months. His eyes sparkled when he talked about the army. He asked me what my dreams were. I answered that I didn't have any. He thought for a long time before he asked me what kind of person I wanted to grow up to be. I replied that I didn't care to be a person, that I'd rather become a carnivorous dinosaur, if possible.

Before he came up with another question, I shot back, "What

were your dreams?"

This succeeded in sending him back to his boyhood. He blinked like a bear that had just emerged from a cave after hibernation. This was a signal that he was traveling to the past. His pupils dilated as if he were in the dark, a sign that his childhood was just as unhappy as any unhappy childhood. It is the same everywhere. Unhappy children's dreams are one and the same: they want to be happy. The abstract doesn't have a thing in common with the concrete. Happiness is the abstract. In other words, happiness has nothing to do with concrete hopes, such as hopes to become a doctor, a lawyer, or a nuclear physicist. He, too, hadn't had any dreams.

"My dream was . . . to fly in the sky like a bird."

See? Dreaming an unrealizable dream was the mark of people who had no choice but to dream in the abstract, not in the concrete.

"Like Icarus?"

"No. Like a bird in the myth. To become a bird whose wings cover the sky."

"You mean the bird that doesn't come to the ground once it soars into the sky? You mean you wanted to die as soon as you started flying."

"You have no manners, kid. Oh, please forgive me, God. If you heard what I saw when I went away with my good Korean friends, you won't be able to go out to the toilet at night."

I wasn't curious. For he was going to lie, without fail. Uncle Amos said he'd gone to a road construction site in Gangwon Province. He helped laying out overpasses and digging tunnels. As his crew dug into the one-third point of the tunnel, they came across a geological stratum from the Neo-cretaceous period. An odd-looking animal, in hibernation, was found there intact. The hungry construction crew scorched the gigantic animal with torches, just as any Korean who killed a dog for food would do. Someone offered sensible advice that a severe beating would make the meat tender, but none of them paid heed because they were exhausted from their hard labor. "As many as fifty people, holding a torch each, worked on the animal. As the body thawed, we began to smell the nauseating stench of scorched hair. And wow! You won't believe this."

The animal woke up. It suddenly opened its bulging eyes, heaved its entire body to shake off the crew, and let out a lion's roar. Just like a cat that was curled up in sleep wakes up and stretches its paws, the round ball of an animal unfurled, with its four limbs all stretched out. Only then could the crew shout, "Dinosaur! Dinosaur! Darn, a dinosaur!"

I was flabbergasted but nodded for his sake. He continued, "You won't believe what happened next. Two excavators and four bulldozers arrived in a hurry. Plus seven dump trucks. Plus a hundred workers or more rushed over, everyone holding a tool. Villagers in the nearby mountain dropped what they were doing and came running. Every one of them carried a shovel, a hoe, or a scythe. And that was it. They all attacked the dinosaur, knocked it down, skinned it like they'd skin a dog, hacked it into chunks, roasted them, and had a feast. If Hassan had been there, he could have shown off his pig-butchering skills. You want to become a carnivorous dinosaur? That kind of dream is hopeless. God wants, at this very moment, that humans lord it over everything. If you become a carnivorous dinosaur, remember to hole yourself up right where you are. Never take a step outside of your home. That's how things stand in the world."

Uncle Amos claimed that the dinosaur meat tasted like a blend of the orangutan, the ostrich, and the sloth. "Anyway, it tasted better than Hassan's pork. That guy is Muslim, so he doesn't know how pork should taste. A man like that selling pork, huh? What can be more ridiculous, I ask?"

When his lies didn't work or he was pushed into a corner, he acted like a homo. Most people grew angrier by his antics, but refrained from becoming violent. They couldn't bring themselves to resort to violence. He whimpered in a high-pitched female voice. Most shrugged or shook their heads and walked away. Those who weren't softened by this tactic faced Aunt Anna's fury. She had an amazing capacity for empathy and identification with a victim. In those moments, at least, she regarded Uncle Amos as a persecuted woman.

"You came to this world with your balls," she'd say to anyone who was about to hit Uncle Amos, "And you try to beat a woman? That shows how pathetic you are!"

Who on this street dared to confront her? They slunk away to avoid being part of a disgraceful scene after the Goddess of Earth, who had curative powers, grabbed them by the throat. When the incident was wrapped up, she clucked her tongue to Uncle Amos and said, "No one can be as nimble as you are. You stretch your private parts sideways to a slit, then you become a woman. You let them go, then you're back to a man."

By then, he was already squatting at the faucet, having rushed out of the kitchen backdoor. He was ready to scrub the gridiron sticky with burnt grease spots. He quipped, "St. Paul said: Those unwilling to work shouldn't stuff themselves with food. Don't interrupt me. You see I'm working, right?"

Aunt Anna said, "Your country doesn't seem to have the saying: you drink kimchi juice in anticipation of rice cake that's not coming your way."

This descendant of Socrates had the talent of letting words go in one ear and right out the other. After some more bitching, Aunt Anna vented her anger on me. "You'll be no different when peach fuzz appears under your nose. You'll fawn over a powerful guy and trample on a weakling. When you're married, you'll beat your woman and then your children . . . Wait, what am I saying to you?"

At a loss, she changed the subject. I was fine. Just my scars prickled. If your children are trouble, you can always abandon them. You just know this without being taught.

Aunt Anna predicted that Uncle Amos would dig his own

grave sooner or later. He lifted his first shovelful one night. He made an X with his arms and reached the hives all over his body and vigorously scratched them. The itching kept him awake all night, so he wandered around the neighborhood. As he passed an unoccupied house, he heard a strange noise.

"I thought youngsters had snuck in," he explained later.

Overcome with curiosity, he stole into the house and put his ear to the door. The low indeterminable sound, which had stopped him in his tracks, drifted out again. When he opened the door, a surprising scene presented itself.

"In that empty house," he said, "a bird is kept. His wings bound by an iron chain, he lives on rain water, wherever it seeps in. The bird's beak and claws are made of steel. His two eyes are gentle but powerful. His chest is thick and fluffy, not a feather missing. His beak can take out Uranus' heart and if a bull is seized by his claws, it will stay right there to the end of the world. But I can't free the bird. No sky's left for him to fly around. Because it's been a long time since humans took over the sky. Sometimes I'm upset to see electric wires crisscrossing above this neighborhood. If we're seen from the sky, we'd look like moths caught in a cobweb, don't you think? What if an angel's wing is caught in the dirty, tangled electric wires?" He said this in a low voice as if revealing a major secret.

That was the end of his antics. He stopped trying to tell lies. Well, he did say that the President would be visiting. Our neighbors didn't believe him, but just in case, they gently polished the picture frames around the President's photo in their homes.

If the bird did exist, that day it must have pecked Uncle Amos in the heart and scratched his soul with its claws.

6

None of the customers at the butcher shop was Muslim. Most of the people who entered the shop were locals or foreigners who weren't Muslims. A money peddler or two hawking daily-interest loans stopped by, and so did the occasional salesman pitching electric meat cutters or industrial-grade refrigerators. Of the customers, the local Koreans pretended they didn't know Uncle Hassan if they ran into him outside his shop. The threshold of the butcher shop wasn't merely a threshold but a border that divided this world from that.

Aunt Anna was the only Korean I knew who treated Uncle Hassan and Uncle Amos the same as she did other people. Her obliviousness was part of it. She didn't dwell on unpleasant experiences, which set her apart. Most people, if they had an unpleasant impression at the sight of Uncle Hassan and Uncle Amos, stored the feeling in their hearts. The first impression, saved this way, was retrieved in their next encounter, kindly telling them how to react to these foreigners. They received a command from their brain, "Don't have anything to do with them!" Aunt Anna might have felt the same way at first, but she soon forgot about it. So she didn't have any fixed notion that prompted her to take a certain attitude.

Yujong was afraid of everyone, so I couldn't tell for sure how he felt about Uncle Hassan and Uncle Amos. This hurt my pride. Yujong was particularly at ease with me because I "wasn't a person," as he put it. This meant that he regarded Uncle Hassan and Uncle Amos at least as members of humanity.

Another person who was similar to Aunt Anna was Smart-aleck. But he was indifferent to everything that went on around him, so it was hard to tell exactly what he thought of Uncle Hassan and Uncle Amos. Smart-aleck regarded them with the same indifference that he showed to the meter reader, the postman, the plainclothes serviceman who went from house to house delivering notifications for the reserve army's exercises, and itinerant vendors who went around selling one useless trinket or another.

Smart-aleck had a friend now. The yellow-striped cat. I wondered whether these two creatures, indifferent to the world, had been husband and wife in their previous lives. He shared the wooden bench with the cat in a companionable manner, and his habits were getting more like the cat's. He slept any time he felt like it and ate any time he felt like it. When he was awake, he moved around vigorously for ten minutes or so, but grew languid like a reptile basking in the sunlight to raise its body temperature. I saw him slowly climbing down the bench on all fours, just like a cat, and crawling into his house. I could bet my life, which was all I had, that a tail would grow on him before long. He and the cat whispered into each other's ear, like the pillow talk between husband and wife. When Yujong appeared, Smart-aleck buried the cat in his arms, like a timid husband before a playboy. His eyes glinting, Smart-aleck warned Yujong, "Don't you dare say a word to my cat!"

Like an experienced scout, the cat darted in and out of the rice shop's inner quarters and reported what the second daughter, the one who resembled a half-eaten *chonggak* kimchi, was up to. Smart-aleck sometimes looked satisfied and at other times depressed, although Yujong didn't interpret for him what the cat said. As far as I knew, Smart-aleck was building up an ability to understand animal language as well.

By the afternoon, strong pork stench permeated the butcher shop so much that even people with the dullest sense of smell weren't immune to it. Uncle Hassan frequently splashed water all over to clean up, but the nauseating sweet smell intensified. I liked to hear the sound of his knife hitting the butcher block. This was different from the rustle Aunt Anna made when she trimmed vegetables or the light taps she created as she cut them up. I could put it this way: Uncle Hassan's sound sent shivers down my spine. Listening to his hacking or slicing meat with my eyes closed, I felt as if my body were being cut up. In one orphanage, I suffered a deep cut from a stationery knife while removing hardened gum stuck to the floor in the hallway outside the office. I still have the scar. The initial pain was instant. I realized that I'd cut myself, but it didn't hurt much. Soon, blood oozed out of the gash, and a smarting sensation surged. As if all the blood in my body had rushed to the cut, my finger felt heavier. As if a heart had sprouted right there, it throbbed. I knew crying was useless. All I could do was put the finger in my mouth and suck in the sticky blood. It tasted like rusted iron. The sensation wasn't unpleasant, but I couldn't shake off the feeling that the blood coursing through my body was rusty. I thought: An orphan received his blood from his parents a long time ago, but there is no flesh and blood to remind him daily of who gave him blood, so he slowly turns rusty.

At the butcher shop, I learned my blood was far from useful. Pig's blood was essential for Aunt Anna. It was a must when making blood sausage soup. But my blood was useful only to me, if it could be called that. If I didn't suck it in, it would go down the drain, swirling in with all the muck.

At dawn, a neighbor we called Baldy sang military songs. For this reason, we thought he wasn't right in the head. I'd been to his house, a bizarre space. Before Baldy moved in, a family of six lived there. The house was adjacent to an alley consisting of stairs. The steep part had narrow stairs and a gentle slope provided what could be called a stairwell every three or four steps. On both sides of the stairwell were doors, too small to be called main entries. They doubled as front and kitchen doors. Entering one of these doors, you'd find yourself smack in the middle of a space holding a coal-briquette stove, a cabinet, and a faucet. This was where people cooked and washed themselves. When a family of six lived at Baldy's, I saw all six entering their home. First, the head of the household went in, soon followed by his wife and then their four children. That seemed to be the order of their entry. When the adults had taken their places, the children slipped in between them. If this order of entry was broken, all had to come out and start all over again. So, they had agreed-on positions and postures just like puzzle pieces, and when they were out of their designated places, it seemed impossible for the six to sleep in the only room they had.

Aunt Anna told me that this family had run away in the middle of the night, shirking the responsibility of six months' rent. This neighborhood wasn't where you could disappear like a plume of smoke, even at night. Someone was always awake. But no one saw them flee, although they gathered up all their belongings before they disappeared, not leaving even a needle behind. Actually, there was a witness, but he'd seen only the father pulling a cart. That was why the witness wasn't suspicious. I believed that the family had fit themselves perfectly to the contours of one another like puzzle pieces, making themselves look like a big load on the cart.

I looked around in their empty room. The space was barely big enough for two adults to lie down. I didn't know how the parents lived in that tiny space with four children, not to mention their household appliances. Under the floor mats, I found a black-and-white photo of the family. It looked like a natural remnant of their life there, not something they'd forgotten. I added the photo to my collection.

Several days after the house became vacant, Baldy moved in. People said he was a distant relative of the landlord. Baldy also brought a cartful of belongings. He skillfully piled up his belongings, leaving just enough space for him to lie down. After arranging his room, he expressed satisfaction, saying that he liked it because the sleeping space was bigger than what he used to have. He added that he'd moved up to a more spacious house. No wonder. Didn't he take the entire six-person space for himself? He babbled about this at the butcher shop. He didn't buy any meat but got some free pork scraps earmarked for Aunt Anna. On the first dawn after his move, he started singing military songs. When his cracking, screeching tune drifted in, Uncle Hassan, sleeping next to me, let out heavy groans. He grunted, shuddered, and talked nonsense in his sleep. I didn't know what gibberish he was saying because he muttered in his native tongue. But I knew what emotion it was freighted with—fear.

Baldy sauntered around the neighborhood during the day, just like a regiment commander making a round of inspections to his subordinate units. I mean, he butted in where he didn't belong. He soon realized that Uncle Hassan's shop was where he could rest his rump and idle away his time because no one paid any attention to the place. Baldy was too mild during the day for anyone to believe that he belted out military songs at the top of his lungs in the early morning hours.

A week after his move, I saw him walking down the side road decked out in a military uniform. To Aunt Anna, who asked where he was headed, he answered that he was off to a meeting to ensure the country's security and future, in a cocky manner befitting a newly minted military official. He looked strapping as any gallant veteran. For him, the military uniform was Samson's hair. His face shone when he wore the uniform. His gait grew measured, his voice dignified, his expression stern. He didn't pick his nose, lift his thigh to release a fart, or block one nostril with his finger before blowing his nose. But Aunt Anna wasn't impressed by anything like military garb. "I've never seen an old guy who didn't claim he was a big fish once upon a time," she said.

Baldy returned with the setting sun draped behind him. His gait was still strong until he entered his house and took off his uniform. When he came out in his usual outfit, he could barely lift his heavy legs to cross the threshold of his door, and appropriated a part of Smart-aleck's bench, where he dozed, hunched over, and let out a pained moan at the slightest touch. He walked bow-legged because of arthritis and hawked up phlegm dozens of times while smoking a single cigarette. Once he started coughing, it escalated into a breathless coughing fit, his face reddening; he cut an ugly figure for sure. He didn't have a wife or children. He couldn't be a wounded soldier because he had no missing body part. He couldn't have been a brave solider because no medal adorned his chest for distinguished military service. Mostly he dozed in front of the butcher shop, and sometimes in front of Aunt Anna's or on Smart-aleck's bench. Then he'd shudder. I, too, shivered from time to time. That was when I had a nightmare.

But mine wasn't a nightmare, precisely. It would be just images of fear. Jolted awake, I couldn't say what had frightened me. I'd touch my brow to discover that a cold sweat had oozed out. I'd wept loudly in my dream, but awake, I couldn't remember what the origins of my sorrow, the object of my fear, had been. I wouldn't have been as scared if there had been monsters or aliens in my dreams. Fear existing only in images was more frightening. It rushed in like a mist and enveloped me like a wind before it ebbed out.

In my dreams, I was sometimes afraid of putting on clothes, eating, or even breathing in and out. Ordinary, natural actions in real life weren't ordinary in my dreams. If I couldn't put on this outfit, then . . . At these moments I was reduced to someone who didn't know how to put on clothes. If I couldn't put on this pair of shoes, then . . . At these moments my feet wouldn't fit into any of thousands of shoes scattered about. If I couldn't eat this rice, then . . . At those moments, rice grains cascaded off my spoon like sand as I kept shoving the empty spoon into my mouth.

No fear of mine was enormous, horrifying, or grand-scale. I'd never dreamed that the earth melted down in a sizzle after the explosion of a nuclear bomb, that a tsunami swallowed an entire city as if it were a piece of candy, or that a Mercury-sized planet collided with the earth, causing a grand explosion. Although my dreams didn't hint at a clear extinction, I was scared because the end seemed imminent. I didn't die, but I felt as if I'd experienced death; I didn't get hurt, but I felt as if I'd just undergone major surgery. So I knew that fear came with a familiar, gentle expression, not in an ugly, disgusting form. That was how fear came to the face of sleeping Baldy. Never was he slowly seized with fear. A sudden shock it was. I could guess that he was having a nightmare. Fear visited only when you were off-guard. That was probably natural. Fear for which you could brace yourself, fear that crept into you, might as well have lost its qualification for being real fear. So fear was something that took you by surprise. Was it because of this reason? People—whoever they were, whether they were foul-tempered or cowardly—looked more good-natured asleep than awake. A person who looked nasty even in sleep had to be evil to the core.

When he was asleep, Baldy looked like a highly disciplined monk. A kind, mild truth-seeker who was ready to teach the masses; a monk enlightened with all the principles of the world and on the verge of self-emancipation.

I told Baldy that his sleeping face looked like a child's. He was taken aback. If someone had said the same thing to me, I'd have reacted the same way. No one has seen his own sleeping face, and no one has felt the need to do so—I guess it will continue to be so—and people don't have a burning curiosity about what their sleeping faces are like. That's why they're astonished when they hear that their sleeping faces look peaceful, sad, or depressed. It's because they realize that they repeatedly put on and take off numerous masks even when they're asleep.

No one had any interest in Baldy. That was expected. He was just one of the hordes of nameless old men around us. Only a few teenage rogues showed flickers of interest because they held him in contempt for being bald and old. At a certain age, do skin colors, races, and nationalities become irrelevant? I couldn't tell exactly why, but I was certain it was so by the time people reached Baldy's age. They wouldn't look out of place if they were parachuted down anywhere in the world. I didn't fully support Aunt Anna's notion that the more you aged, the uglier you became on account of God's curse lest you should dream of eternal life. My argument was: What about people who were born ugly? What are they supposed to do? Just because they are ugly doesn't guarantee longevity. Still, people tend to identify appearances that have grown ugly with souls that have grown ugly.

That was the way of God. When three old men—Uncle Hassan, Uncle Amos, and Baldy, who wouldn't be expected to be in the same place normally—were together, I wondered whether they'd grown up as bosom buddies and were getting old together. I had a feeling that the trio had been together in the past, wherever it might have been.

Baldy often egged on Uncle Amos. He believed that he could excite two people—the boy Amos and the girl Anna—with dirty jokes and by pushing Uncle Amos from behind, encouraging him to be bold. His attempt failed every time. He changed his target and used the same tactic for Smart-aleck, but the boy fainted at Baldy's lewd suggestions. The yellow-striped cat crouched, as if a tombstone, on the stomach of the fallen boy. Baldy succeeded in exciting the boy, but it was too much of a success. The boy was pushed into an intense excitement, which escalated until his body collapsed. He suffered from a high fever for three days running. Baldy visited him every day.

The boy's parents didn't welcome his visits but gladly accepted his gifts: a bottle of honeyed water, soft drinks, pastries, cookies, caramels, or English candies. The comforting offerings by Baldy were distributed to me and Yujong because the boy who wished to die had no interest in them. Smart-aleck's eyes glinted with anger. He forced himself to taste a cookie, but that was it; he must have tasted only bitterness. He was deep in thought, probably plagued with a depressing thought that if he died, he'd be as lonely as a naked soldier left behind on the battlefield in ancient times, even the clothes on his back stolen.

Who cares if you die? Then all your belongings will be mine. To make him understand this, I made a show of relishing his goodies.

With the fever gone, Smart-aleck became a different person. He was indifferent to whatever Yujong and I suggested.

"Down there, there's a huge ash tree. It's so big that it can be Yggdrasill, you'll see. If you go down there, you'll meet a wise man waiting to impart his wisdom."

"Who cares? I'm going to die."

"Yujong found an amazing animal. It has a single eye, right in the middle of his forehead. He must be a Cyclops under the magic spell that will shrink his body. You want to see him, right?"

"Who cares? I'm going to die."

"If you clamp down the backs of your sneakers with your heels like that, they won't last long."

"Who cares? I'm going to die."

"Look! Isn't this book amazing?"

"Who cares? I'm going to die."

"Let's meet here again after lunch."

"Who cares? I'm going to die."

"Gosh, you can die when the time comes, but how about you do what you have to before you die?"

"Who cares? I'm going to die."

Smart-aleck had lost his sense of humor. He was an actor in a tragedy with a comedian's face.

Baldy thought that Smart-aleck was the feeblest of us three. He assured us that with his military-style training he'd whip the boy into shape, making him a real man.

"A donkey can sprint toward a hill like a wild horse if I train it. Don't worry. I'll make you a vigorous youth of the Republic of Korea."

Both Baldy and Smart-aleck were the type of people who'd be exhausted after a ten-minute stretching exercise. When they were together, they'd listlessly look up to the sky or sit blankly. Nothing had changed.

But Smart-aleck said otherwise. "Actually, I'm changed. I'm not anxious when I'm with Grandfather Baldy. Yes, that's what's changed. Now I know what it really was, the sadness I felt that used to paralyze me. You know what? It was my anxious mind, not knowing what to do because I didn't know why I was so sad. That feeling led to anxiety, and the anxious mind, ever more anxious, fed on my existing anxiety. Just like two mirrors reflecting each other, twins of anxiety copied each other and multiplied."

But as far as I was concerned, Baldy and Smart-aleck had grown doubly bored, that was all.

Squatting before the locksmith, I pointed to Baldy and Yujong as they passed by. "Who are they?"

"Elephants."

"What kind of elephants?"

"Pink elephants."

"Gosh. Isn't there a blue elephant or a yellow elephant?"

"Pink elephants."

"Okay. What are they doing?"

"Passing by."

"Where are they headed?"

He didn't say anything.

7

Uncle Hassan renewed his efforts to find a school for me. Customers dwindled at his shop in the aftermath of a sweeping hog cholera. Chunks of meat continued to age in the freezer and only swarms of flies buzzed in the shop. When Uncle Hassan threw in an extra portion with a purchase, the customer grew suspicious, asking if it was from a carcass afflicted with hog cholera. Uncle Hassan said that he could tell whether the animal had come down with cholera, but none believed him. Dispirited, he returned home for a prayer and lunch before going back to his shop. He stayed there, though no one entered, until late into the evening. On Fridays, he closed his store and went off somewhere and brought brochures for alternative schools. Whenever I spotted a brochure, I took out a match from the fat UN Match box and burned it.

I knew how hypocritical any belief was, but I believed what Uncle Amos said: a gigantic bird that had a steel beak and claws was bound by an iron chain.

No one believed an orphan. Yet, people always claimed that they did. It was the same in every orphanage. The directors said that they believed we'd grow up to be the pillars of our country.

People who brought goods for us said that they believed we'd grow up to be great talents. Yet no one truly believed it.

I glimpsed contempt in their eyes, as if they were looking at mutated creatures that shouldn't have been born. Some eyes were filled with affection and sympathy, but when we spat at them or defied them, their affection and sympathy disappeared in a flash. Theirs was cheap affection and sympathy that could be withdrawn at any time unless we were obedient.

At an orphanage, the director and his wife exchanged an unfunny joke about me. "He must've been a handful. Look how violent his parents were to him!"

"It's fair to say that with a scar like that, they wanted to kill him."

They tittered, looking at the scar below my right collarbone. Poking fun at the wounded is a talent only humans possess.

I didn't want to possess anything. I couldn't own any of the things, anyway. Socks, underwear, pants, sneakers, and school supplies were given to me, but I had them only provisionally; they didn't completely belong to me. People tested us to see if we were duly qualified to have them. To pass the test, we were not to avert our eyes or let our attention drift when they were talking to us, and we were not to go against their wishes or show our defiance. We were supposed to use only the words they taught us and we were not to crave more than they gave us. We were to follow their orders and accept their punishment with a glad heart. What was most frustrating for me was that I was supposed to be grateful to these people. I was thankful, all right, because they didn't allow me to forget, even for a moment, what kind of a person I was.

People who ran an orphanage or anyone involved with it seemed to have received special training. Do Not Trust Orphans: This seemed to be the title of the manual they'd been trained with.

One day, I spotted the orphanage director's ring on the edge of a bathroom sink. This incident took place at the last orphanage I was in. He usually wore this thick, ugly ring on his pinky.

Engraved on it were Republic of Korea and Loyalty. He held this ring dear to his heart because the ring proved that he'd been part of the military. He didn't wear it every day, but he made sure to put it on when civil servants or sponsors came to visit. On days he wore it, we knew that we'd have visitors.

He gathered us orphans together and without a word slapped each of us across the cheek. He slapped those of us who generally rubbed him the wrong way a few more times. I received three slaps. Afterward, he explained, in a sad tone, why he'd been compelled to resort to violence. *I trusted you guys. I considered you my own children. But how ungrateful can you get? My ring is important. You all know that, don't you? Hiding that ring is the same as betraying your country.* As always, his speech ended with a threat.

He used the method he'd always employed when he was in the army. He made us close our eyes and ordered that the child who'd taken his ring raise his hand. Not a single hand shot up. He asked us to put our heads on our desks, eyes closed. He ordered that the one who'd taken his ring stand up quietly. No one stood up. He didn't lose his calm. It appeared that his competitive spirit was flaring up in the face of a worthy opponent. He walked over to a five-year-old girl. He told her to open her eyes and asked if she knew who'd taken it. She was a good child in the true sense of the word. She said she didn't know. The director didn't believe her. He was faithful to the manual. It didn't matter whether or not the girl was good. *You are not to believe an orphan's words in any circumstance.* He asserted that he'd seen her in the hallway just outside the bathroom. She said she'd never been there. He asked, Then whose is this red hair band? He was holding a cheap article. The girl burst into tears. He held her gently, as if embracing his own child. Stroking her hair, he assured her that it was okay. *I know you didn't steal it. So be honest. Now, who stole it? Yes, you're a good girl. I trust you.* To him, trust was another form of mistrust.

I knew that in desperation she'd point at anyone. I knew how insulting it was to be pinned down like that. I'd been picked out several times in similar situations. I also knew how horrifying it was to point to someone at random. I knew a boy who'd gone crazy after he'd done just that.

I raised my hand: "I stole it!" The director turned his head to gaze at me. I saw his mask slipping off. As his hidden face was revealed, a cruel smile danced around his mouth. He ordered me to put forth his ring. I pointed to the fence. *Are you saying you threw it over the fence? You threw my precious ring on the dirty grass out there? If I don't find my ring right there, get ready for what's coming to you. You'd better pray I'll find my ring.*

He drove all the orphans out to the grass. I pretended I was searching. I saw a boy who was two years older than me drop the ring at his foot through his pant leg. He'd run away several times to look for his parents but had been brought back from the bus terminal every time. His parents were alive. With that fact alone, he was the envy of other orphans. He might have thought that the ring would translate into his bus fare. He'd been brought back from the terminal because no nice person bought him a ticket. He shouted that he found the ring. The director walked over to take the ring back. He kissed it and wrapped it in his handkerchief before putting it in his pant pocket.

I was left all alone in the front yard. It was time for punishment. That was when I saw a man shuffling through the front gate. If there was a monster that devoured only orphans, it would probably look like him, I decided. That was Uncle Hassan.

He looked at me standing all alone. I didn't run away at the sight of the stranger, unlike the other children, not because the director had ordered me to stay right there. I could have easily ignored his order and taken cover. Uncle Hassan's gaze—it was what I'd never experienced before, something mysterious. His gaze looked as if pain, sorrow, joy, or happiness had never stayed there, and it had no need to look at things because everything he had to look was in his own eyes.

A little later, the director called me inside. The ring shone, nastily, on his pinky. Uncle Hassan didn't pay attention to what the director was saying. His eyes stroked me. And I let him run his rough hand over me, as if I were a marionette. His hand conveyed loneliness.

"How do you know the general? He's one of our sponsors, you know," the director said.

Uncle Hassan didn't hear him.

"I heard about your distinguished valor during the war. We're always grateful. If another war breaks out, our business will thrive. Because for us there'll be more orphans to take care of..."

The director realized that Uncle Hassan was glaring at him. "So, anyway, please put in a good word for me with the general."

This was when the director commented that I was stupid. That he was doubtful whether my seed was even Korean. He didn't seem to have any notion that his remark might offend Uncle Hassan.

"You know that we don't accept returns, right? If this kid misbehaves or turns out to be a handful, a juvenile delinquent, we have no responsibility for that."

The director bent his knees to hug me. The disgusting smell of his hair attacked me. I averted my face. Uncle Hassan looked down at me with patient eyes.

"Be a good boy and do as he says," the director said. "Otherwise, I'll come and you'll be in big trouble." He guffawed.

I decided to learn that laugh. I wished I'd have an opportunity to make him hear the same laugh one day.

Uncle Hassan, ignoring the director, told me, "Child, don't be so hateful. None of us alive today will breathe a hundred years from now. All of us must leave this place, leaving behind the beautiful sky, earth, and loved ones."

I can't say his words particularly comforted me or moved me. But no one had told me anything like that before. But for his words, I wouldn't have followed him out so meekly.

While waiting for our bus at the terminal, I asked Uncle Hassan which general the director had been referring to and how he knew the general.

"I don't know him. The imam knows him."

I had no idea who the imam was or what it meant. I just assumed it was someone's name.

"But why did you take me out?"

"I asked the imam and he asked the retired general. The retired general must have told the director. That he should send you out with me."

"This is not right."

"Right or wrong—this is not a matter for you to judge yet. The imam is also on the steering committee at another orphanage. You officially belong to that orphanage, so there's no problem."

"Then you're not adopting me."

"I couldn't even if I wanted to."

"Why are you taking me?"

He didn't answer. That was fine. There was no need to awkwardly call someone Father or Mother.

"Then I can call you Uncle, right? Or do you want me to call you Grandfather?"

After a slight pause, he said, "As you wish."

After I began to live with Uncle Hassan, I wondered all the time. Why did he bring me home with him? There were many better-looking, obedient boys and cute, docile girls. Seeing him tormented in sleep at the sound of Baldy's military songs and realizing that he was eyeing my scars with pity, I ventured a guess: He must have done something awful on the battlefield, maybe killing a boy soldier my age or smashing the skull of a man whose name happened to be the same as mine.

When Aunt Anna laid eyes on me, she asked Uncle Hassan if I was the boy. So she'd heard about me. I asked her why I'd been brought there. She was caught off-guard. "That old guy must have wanted a son who'll take care of him in his old age. He'll plump you up and then kill you to eat. So be careful. When he holds a knife, don't go near him. Okay?" She then howled like an angry tiger with the typical gesture grownups use to scare children. I mean, she raised her palms next to her face, made quick fists and opened them. She believed that kids were to be teased, for only then could they grow up sound and healthy.

I thought I'd find out nothing from her. Asking Uncle Amos was exhausting because he lied all the time. He said, "No one can tell what that filthy Turk is thinking. Even God will shake his head about the guy—Oh, forgive me, God!—well, let's see. Nothing about you looks like him. So don't you worry. A terrible misfortune veered away from you. You can't be a hidden son or a grandson of that filthy Turk."

Whatever relationship Uncle Hassan and Uncle Amos had, it couldn't have been an entirely pleasant one. I had no idea why a Turk and a Greek had to come all the way here to bicker over everything. If I was forced to choose the grouchier between the two, it was Uncle Amos, hands down.

"Uncle Amos, why did you come to this country?"

He thought for a minute. As if he were dredging up something he'd forgotten for a long time. "Because I killed my uncle."

I mimicked the tone of retired generals I'd seen on television. "You were in a war. Everyone knows something like that happens all the time during the war. Forget all about it."

"I killed my aunt, too."

"It must have been a mistake."

"Yes, it was a mistake. I made one mistake too many. I also killed my cousins. I killed the entire family. My flesh and blood at that. Every single member of the family, the children of people who called me their nephew, the parents of the children who called me their cousin."

For goodness's sake! So, Uncle Amos was a bloodthirsty murderer, ruthless and cruel!

Next to us, Aunt Anna muttered, "Now I know why he couldn't

live in his country. Is this country the world's public toilet? All those cruel thugs coming in droves! I knew it! When he brandishes a swatter, he catches two flies at a time. That's a talent, all right." Aunt Anna's joke didn't work. Uncle Amos's face was still long.

I asked, "All the foreign soldiers who came here during the Korean War, were they all fugitives like you?"

He nodded listlessly. Preoccupied with his own thoughts, it seemed he didn't hear my question.

"What about Uncle Hassan? Did he spray bullets at a whole family to erase them from the face of the earth, and then come here?"

"He could have done that, right?" He asked as if he were curious about that, too. Then he shook his head. "My people banded together and fought against Hitler and Mussolini. My father and his younger brother were famous guerrillas. So was my aunt. The underground wedding of my uncle and my aunt was the talk of the town at the time and all youngsters dreamed of fighting for freedom and independence and falling in love, just like them. The three of them—my father, uncle, and aunt—had been on the brink of hell so many times that it looked as if death, not their shadows, was hanging around them. The war ended and peace came. Everyone believed so. But my uncle went up to the mountains. He became a partisan. I was flying an old plane provided by America, one that had been used during the Second World War. My father was a regional commander of the royal army. My uncle, on the other hand, was the leader of the region's partisans. My father didn't do it in the open but secretly looked after my aunt and her children."

After the Second World War, Greece was engulfed in civil war. On one of the final days of the war, Uncle Amos sat in the cockpit of an outdated P-40. His dream of flying had come true, finally. On that day, he didn't know what his mission was.

"Maintaining the altitude and keeping the radio on, I waited for an order to come through. I knew it couldn't be bombing because no bombs had been loaded, but I wasn't sure if it would be simple reconnaissance. No pilot welcomed an order to bomb. There wasn't a psycho among us who enjoyed civil war. We wanted the war to end as soon as possible, that was all. As I entered a zone that had good visibility, I realized that I was flying over my hometown, in the sky I'd looked up to every day as a child. The royal army was in control there; the partisans had been already swept away. A few days before my sortie, I went to see my aunt and cousins. All were worried about what would happen to my uncle. My father reassured my aunt that after the war he would do his best to secure my uncle's amnesty. I knew that my father wasn't convincing. My uncle wouldn't have accepted pardon, mindful of his colleagues who'd been killed. We all knew that he'd rather kill himself when the moment came than become a prisoner of the government army. But what else could my father say in that situation? I felt defiant toward my father, but felt deep sympathy at the same time. If I'd been in a situation where I had no choice but to say something like that, I would have died of anguish."

The young pilot Amos was overjoyed when he learned that his mission was reconnaissance. Just like any other young men, he wanted to show off to the residents in his hometown. He lowered his altitude to the point of scraping the belfry of the village church. He waved at the priest, who was leaving the taverna, the village eatery. The priest, of course, was shocked to see a plane flying toward him, so he threw himself flat on the ground. His hat flew off and rolled down the street. The young Amos laughed heartily. After passing over the village, he was about to turn the nose of his plane. It was then that his plane was shot at by machine guns.

"That happened from time to time. Partisans would sneak into the royal army's bastion to see their families or get supplies of food and weapons. I thought the partisans had shot me. My plane was an old type, so it had a total of four machine guns mounted on the main wings. It was easy to find my attackers. They weren't under cover. I immediately turned the plane's nose toward them and, approaching, I strafed . . . It was too late when I noticed that they were civilians. I don't know why they ran out from behind a rock where they were hiding." Uncle Amos' eyes were red by now.

"You couldn't have known who they were."

"Yes, I could. Someone standing on the rock waved his handkerchief. I was flying a single-engine prop plane. The handkerchief flew away after the person was shot, and it was blown into my propeller and stuck there. After I landed, I found the tattered handkerchief. It was my birthday gift to my cousin. His initials were embroidered on it."

After the civil war, Uncle Amos went home. Then he escaped his village as if running away. When a war broke out in Korea, he volunteered to the Greek unit that was to be dispatched there. He wanted to flee to the farthest corner of the earth possible. That was how he came to this country of pungent soybean paste, located practically on the other side of the globe. Ah Uncle, you came too far, I thought.

"The worst mistake I made was I used the war as a refuge." He shut his eyes firmly. Tears seeped out from the corners of his eyes. Then he fell asleep. Just as he'd done at home a long time ago, he drifted off to a siesta.

8

One evening, all hell broke loose at the rice store.

By then, Smart-aleck had cut off his lingering attachment to the rice store's second daughter. When all was said and done, Baldy was responsible for this change of heart. Baldy, Smart-aleck, and the yellow-striped cat formed a landscape of their own, and taking them apart seemed impossible. Baldy promised that he'd help Smart-aleck find love.

Smart-aleck was indifferent even to that. "Who cares? I'm going to die."

Baldy cajoled him with all kinds of sweet talk.

"Who cares? I'm going to die."

"That's the right attitude. What'd be impossible if you charged forward with that attitude?"

Soon enough, the rice store's daughter, the one who looked like a half-eaten *chonggak* kimchi, passed by. Smart-aleck climbed down off the bench with the attitude of *who cares? I'm going to die,* and called out to her. He walked over to her like a regular verb but burst into tears like an irregular adjective. He might have hated it more than anything else in the world.

Since the person who was supposed to confess his love started sobbing like a baby, it was a big letdown for us onlookers. Even the locksmith grinned. The rice store's daughter dealt Smart-aleck deadly blows. Right then and there, he became the recipient of scathing swear words, ten times more in quantity than he'd heard since birth. Her last remark wasn't necessarily a curse, but it was no different from the final blow. "Hey, you sure you're a boy, not a girl?"

From then on, Smart-aleck would refuse to look in the direction of the rice store. He would rot to the core with his chastity intact. The girl walked away, laughing merrily. Like father, like daughter. The rice seller Kim was a walking dictionary of swear words. When he opened his mouth, even passing dogs staggered back in shock. To curse someone, he summoned all types of dogs in the world to our neighborhood. Dog this, dog that, dog here, dog there . . . He was notorious for his sleight of hand, deceiving his customers with his scale or sneaking fillers into his rice, just like petty government officials in charge of grain loans during the Joseon dynasty. The customers who had bought rice from him or sold it to him would come back to protest belatedly, long after the transactions were over; loud voices, curses, and scuffles were routine affairs at his shop. The poor residents in our area didn't buy rice in large quantities at a time. They bought it by the size of a letter envelope or a document envelope. On the evening I'm talking about, a disgruntled customer didn't have the nerve to have it out with Kim all by himself, so he came with the proselytizer leading the way.

Now Kim encountered a new type of opponent. The proselytizer stood his ground against Kim, armed with endurance and faith. Kim brought out his opponent's grandfathers going back eight generations and cursed them in the name of all the dogs in the world, but he couldn't drive away the proselytizer, who, on bent knees, was praying before him. Kim must have been seized with a sudden fear. He pretended to feel dizzy, placing his palm on his forehead, and called out to his daughters. Kim's three daughters acted as a stretcher to lug him inside. The proselytizer approached the door of the inner quarters on his knees and prayed in a louder voice. Now he began to shower curses on Kim. All kinds of hell in the universe were summoned to that door.

It dawned on Kim that the situation was turning more disadvantageous for him. So he dragged Uncle Hassan, who was at the butcher shop, into the scene.

"I have a bad headache. I'm dizzy. I'm nauseated. I'm dying." Kim made a self-diagnosis, claiming that he got sick from the pork in the kimchi stew he'd eaten for dinner. Kim sent all his family members to the butcher shop.

"Hog cholera, perhaps?" One of the onlookers ventured cautiously. That was exactly what Kim was angling for.

"Yes, yes. I bet it's hog cholera. I heard it's contagious," someone else chimed in. People backed away from the rice store. The proselytizer was still heaping curses on Kim.

Kim said in irritation, "Hey, Mr. Proselytizer. How about cursing the Turk who sold me the damn pork?"

Uncle Hassan threw an indifferent look at the people streaming into his shop. While walking from the rice store to the butcher shop, many wondered whether they'd contracted the disease. This suspicion churned their stomachs and spun their heads. The power of imagination!

Uncle Hassan had been in low spirits because he couldn't send me to school. He couldn't make heads or tails of what the people piling into his shop were talking about. When he didn't show any response, they decided he was guilty. One of them took out a lump of pork from the display case and slammed it on the chopping board. Someone took up a knife, cut a piece from the lump, and threw it at Uncle Hassan. All these poor people were filled with anticipation. Uncle Hassan was perplexed.

"Eat it if it's not infected with hog cholera," a man in the group demanded and everyone agreed that it was a great idea.

I weaved through the crowd and stood beside Uncle Hassan.

He shuddered just like when he heard Baldy's military songs. This old man, weathered by all sorts of storms in life, and a hulking man at that, failed to say anything, with his fingers and mouth trembling.

The healing of scars is suspended this way. The wounded pretend to be fine, trying to forget about it as soon as possible, but can't be freed from other people's eyes. Before a wound is healed another one comes along. When wounds multiply this way, one's entire body is covered with scars. From this moment on, we start paying someone back with wounds. But Uncle Hassan wasn't one who'd pay anyone back even if it meant he would physically break. I knew that his failure to put in a word of rightful protest was proof he was accustomed to tolerating pain. But this was a common exception. People gathered at his shop were also used to getting hurt but clumsy about hurting others.

I picked up the piece of pork and put it on a scale, the pink flesh that looked like a uvula someone had just thrown up. The spring of the scale jumped. All eyes were on the scale. One hundred grams of sorrow. My palms felt clammy and slippery. I picked up the meat and tossed it into my mouth. A strong meat odor flooded into my mouth. A whiff of sourness and unpleasant sweetness coming from the raw meat. I felt like throwing up. Bloody juice, diluted with saliva, started dripping from the corners of my mouth. The meat was too tough to be cut into smaller pieces. I clamped it down on my molars and managed to tear out a piece. As I chewed, several people retched. With politeness verging on brazenness, I studied those gathered there. If I could, I wanted to cut out all their faces and put them in my scrapbook. I chewed on and on until people turned around, by ones and twos, and slipped out, leaving only the two of us behind. The meat was moving around on my palate and tongue and between my teeth.

I willed that I could swallow it. I willed that it would be digested inside me to become a nutrient that would fill up the dented surfaces of my scars. The light from the red-cellophane-covered bulbs caressed Uncle Hassan's distorted face, dismally and pathetically. The butcher shop closed its doors. Uncle Hassan said this was only temporary. Aunt Anna complained because she had to walk farther to get ingredients for her blood sausage soup. The rice seller Kim was fine. Instead, the proselytizer took to his bed. He came down with a fever, his throat swollen and stamina wiped out after spewing out so many curses in one sitting.

I kept all the doors open in the house. It was inconvenient because Smart-aleck's mutterings came in clearly, but I couldn't stand the revolting pork stink that permeated the house. After swallowing the morsel of pork, I'd thrown up everything, even what was in the rectum, it seemed. If I retched a little longer, my anus would have jumped out of my mouth. Uncle Hassan took out all the clothes, including those in the wardrobe, and washed them. Even those that had been buried deep in the wardrobe were dragged out. A faint smell of mothballs circled the tip of my nose. Referring to me, Uncle Amos, clucking his tongue, said, "Even God can't deter an idiot."

The military uniform hanging on the clothesline looked ancient and faded. Attached to the jacket's right arm was a crescent and a star. On the left arm was a trace of something that had been torn off. This had to be where the rank mark used to be. The pants were baggy around the knees and the hems were so ragged that they looked like a circus clown's fringed pants. A squashed military hat and combat boots had been also taken out. There was so much washing to do that he had to stop in the middle for his prayer.

Uncle Hassan didn't say anything. It was a clear day without a speck of cloud. In our room bathed in the sunlight, chips of lime, dried out and loosened like old scabs, fell from the whitewashed bricks in a trail of specks, as flimsy as a dragonfly's wing. I was drained. My head spun. I could feel the earth rotating as I lay immobile. I was ashamed, too. The night before, I cried like an idiot in Uncle Hassan's arms. I didn't expect the word would jump out of my mouth: Mom. Like a fool, crying and calling out Mom. I'd never missed Mom and I'd never cried like that before. But then here I was, weeping and calling Mom in the arms of the old hulking Turk.

I could still feel the squishy pork in my mouth. Even my tongue felt foreign. I rinsed out my mouth as often as I could and brushed my teeth with a lot of toothpaste, but the smell and the sensation didn't subside. I was also revolted by the kebabs Uncle Hassan made. He said, "After you burn your mouth with hot milk, you blow even on cold yogurt. Don't force yourself to eat yet. Time will make you feel better."

My intestines were completely empty. My body was a void filled with sadness. Uncle Hassan would stop his washing and come over to touch my forehead or rub my stomach with his wet hand. I said I was fine. The scar under my collarbone did smart, as if a hook had raked through it. He eyed my scar and looked away. I touched my scar. It felt as if bloody pus was oozing out, but it was as it had always been—my scar whose origins I didn't know. I didn't remember, but would my body remember it? The scars on my body were records of my sad past. They were evidence that my soul had been tortured. My body remembered the pain forgotten by my soul. How remarkable the human body was!

I asked Uncle Hassan whether he had a scar somewhere on his body, a scar only he knew about. Without glancing at me, he said, "No one in the world is without scars. All wounds leave scars no matter how well they're treated. The world is a bramble of people, so it's impossible not to get hurt even if you stay on this planet only briefly."

"Don't be vague. Just tell me if you have a scar or not."

"Why wouldn't I have one? I have many, actually. Some are faint and some are vivid, but... Don't be obsessed with scars. Your scars want you to be obsessive, because the more obsessed you are, the longer they'll last."

"Do you know something about this scar? I have a feeling that you do."

I wondered myself why I was so obsessed with this particular one. When I thought of it, I felt betrayed. It was a similar sense of betrayal a teenage boy might feel before the mirror about his face that didn't shine no matter how much he primped.

Uncle Amos, claiming that it was a Greek remedy, made me drink some mysterious liquid. Later I learned that it was sugared Korean rice wine. I managed to drink a few sips but soon my stomach hurt as if I'd swallowed a bunch of tacks. When I threw up the mysterious liquid, Uncle Amos expressed regret about the waste.

Aunt Anna shooed him away and put down a bowl of rice porridge near my head. "Sometimes, foolish guys forget they're human and swallow something that's for lions and tigers. I've never seen any guy who didn't get sick afterward. Guys are a strange tribe. All of them are foolish—children, adults, old men, all of them. Now, try to have a little bit of this. It will settle your stomach."

I was revolted by the smell of sausage soup exuding from the pores of her body. When I started gagging and heaving, she clucked her tongue and went away. I was disconcerted. I heard that at one point Uncle Amos had lived with a Korean woman who was manic-depressive. Aunt Anna asked him what it was like to live with someone like that. He shrugged and said: It's easy if you pretend you're living with a drunk all day long. Whatever she said, however she acted, you accept that it isn't strange for a drunk to do that.

Uncle Hassan sharpened an old military jackknife. I dropped off to sleep to the sound of grinding,

I was jolted awake by a nightmare. The shriek in my dream turned out to be Baldy's song. It was the first time that he was singing in the middle of the day.

"When we sang this song, we could advance tall, not ducking, even when bullets showered like rain drops. What do you think?

Isn't this a great song?"

As Baldy opened his mouth to resume the song, Uncle Hassan waved his hand to stop him. Pointing to the military uniform hanging on the line, Baldy said triumphantly, "We used to cheer when we saw that flag. But it's strange. Was the crescent down there like that? Let me see."

Uncle Hassan spoke grumpily. "The ay-yildiz has a crescent at the left-top corner and a star to its right."

"Yes, that's right. If you turn it clockwise, you get the moon-star flag. Anyway, it was amazing. Whenever we spotted a moon-star flag, we shouted, Turkish soldiers! Soldiers from our brother country! You remember that, too, don't you? The time you crushed the dirty Chinese at Gunu-ri. It was amazing. At close quarters . . . "

Uncle Hassan corrected him in a dismal voice. "No. The Gunu-ri battle was a disgrace that couldn't and shouldn't have happened to Muslims. We pulled back without an order, driving numerous fellow warriors to death."

To me, they sounded as if they were discussing a typhoon that had swept through the city the year before.

"Then was it the Yongin battle? At Gamnyangjang, you conquered the high hill in a hand-to-hand engagement. That's correct, right?"

"You're right. But that wasn't an exploit to brag about, either. We charged toward the enemy when they were stupefied from a relentless assault from U.S. bombers."

"But how come you don't have a medal? The bravery shown by the Turks at Gamnyangjang was legendary even after the war. I thought all the soldiers who participated in the battle received a medal for their valor."

Uncle Hassan vigorously shook out my pants that he'd just rinsed. Baldy's face was spattered with water drops as if they were bullets from a machine gun. Baldy, covered in imaginary holes, died in action. This was how grownups continued to play war.

Out on the street, Smart-aleck tickled a dew claw of the yellow-striped cat. The cat, eyes closed, purred. Yujong brought a drawing that depicted the imagined primitive man.

"I . . . I thought you, you'd li . . . like it."

I told him I liked it. Yujong insisted on interpreting the cat's words, although Smart-aleck blocked his ears. Smart-aleck pretended that he wasn't listening to what Yujong had to say, claiming that he, too, understood the cat.

"The se . . . second daughter of the rice, rice store, ran away . . . agai . . . again." Smart-aleck took his fingers away from his ears and blew on them, flicking away the earwax smeared on his nail.

"This, this time . . . she, she left a le . . . letter. She may . . . never come back."

"Huh. Who cares? I'm going to die," Smart-aleck replied.

"You . . . you haven't thou . . . thought about . . . it?" Yujong's inflection was lifted. This meant he was getting worked up. "Dying . . . means ruin. It means you . . . you can't see that, that beautiful long hair again. If be . . . beautiful things disappear, wh . . . what are our eye . . . eyes for? We have eyes to . . . to see them."

Yujong empathized with disappearing things. He talked about how soft it felt when he stroked the cat, how regular and quiet the throbs came when he put his hand under the purring cat's chin, and how mildly ticklish he felt when the cat licked the back of his hand. He talked about the curve of the cat's back when she stretched her limbs as far as they could go, about the crouching posture she struck when she was dozing with her chin resting on her front folded paws, and about the gleam in her eyes when looking at a target as she swayed side to side right before she made a leap. Then he mentioned how all these disappeared in a flash, and how nothing was everlasting.

"Who cares? I'm going to die."

Yujong was silent. He was thinking very hard about how imprecise language was. He thought that no verbal expression could describe anything, actually. That was his dilemma.

"Language can't express everything, but there must be things that have to be expressed," I offered.

Yujong didn't nod readily. I knew that he wasn't born with a speech impairment. He wasn't mute like the priest who'd been from a mining village and he didn't have problems with his tongue or vocal cords. He was simply fearful. He wasn't convinced that the words he used could be conveyed to the listener as he intended. He was afraid and suspicious of people who verbalized everything. He was also afraid and suspicious of people who didn't take into consideration that language could turn into a sharp arrow and inflict harm on the listener. Yujong was genuinely afraid of others but couldn't really hold them in contempt. Those who could only be fearful of others had no choice but to direct their contempt to themselves. Yujong said that he hated himself so much that it was unbearable. He didn't know what a lovely person he was. Whenever he spoke, I saw sunrays dancing over a water fountain. I saw Yujong's words, each and every one of them, floating in the air in its own color, just like transparent baubles that showered down all together, like a moment when each drop of water, pregnant with the sunlight, sparkled as a world of its own. Even the repeated syllables in his stammers differed in color. When he said, *D . . . Da . . . Dammit,* I heard *Damn, Daaamn, and Daaaammit.* When he spoke, I felt as if a rainbow hung from his mouth. My language, indifferent to the point of being monotonous, was lifeless, and so was most of the language spoken by our neighbors, including Aunt Anna; Uncle Hassan's and Uncle Amos' language was similar to Yujong's. Metaphorically speaking, theirs was impudent language, just like a bullet that struck the target before exploding.

Yujong was a sort of perfectionist. He quickly erected a linguistic barrier while hesitating, and stared at how the words he'd fired were conveyed to the listener, just like Balkan people who kept an eye on bandits through a bullet hole they'd created in their wall. Yujong was a person who hid himself under his tongue. Rather than being a person who mistrusted the accuracy of language, he was closer to a person who was mesmerized by the inaccuracy of language.

Smart-aleck didn't understand Yujong's silence. As was the case with people like him, he couldn't tolerate silence.

"Who cares? I'm going to die. All I have to do is be reborn. It's the same with the rice store's second daughter. We can even say what she did is desirable. It's abnormal if you don't go astray in this troubled world. I don't care if she returns or not. No one can meddle with another person's fate."

Yujong let out a sigh. If he could stammer a sigh, he would have done so. "Lem . . . let me tell . . . tell you something. Your cat said . . . said she wi . . . will stick to you un . . . until she dies. So . . . so don't be scared, the cat says. She does . . . doesn't mind how your fate turns out. She'll go . . . go a . . . along with your fate."

Smart-aleck was going to torment himself all night. His brain would be on the verge of paralysis because "doesn't mind how your fate turns out" could mean the cat would turn a blind eye to whichever direction his fate took or it could mean that she wouldn't turn a blind eye even if his fate was wretched. Like Yujong, Smart-aleck would be mesmerized by the inaccuracy of language. Just because we don't stammer doesn't mean that our souls are full of conviction.

Smart-aleck climbed down from the bench. Baldy, decked out in military uniform, instructed his subordinate in front of his house in a confident manner like an active soldier who'd just received an order.

"Obedience, obedience, obedience. That's A to Z. Got it?" Baldy was nervous. He wasn't sure if he could trust Smart-aleck. He thought the boy needed training.

"From this moment on," said Baldy, "you're It. Where am I now?" He was afraid that he'd lose Smart-aleck in a crowded place. So in the name of training, he had crawled under the bench.

His face registering disbelief, Smart-aleck said, "What? Who cares? I'm going to die."

Baldy repeated this game of hide-and-seek. He concealed himself here and there, but he moved slowly and a part of him was always exposed, so Smart-aleck discovered him every time. Baldy was satisfied by his own intentional mistakes. He thought that he'd instilled enough confidence in the boy, and went for an excursion accompanied by this subordinate of his. An old man in military garb and a prematurely aged boy, hand in hand, walked down the side road. Their different gaits prevented them from falling into step, so theirs was far from a majestic march. In a surprising gesture, Baldy took off his field cap and put it on Smart-aleck's head. With this, they seemed to seal a pact.

After they left, I stayed in bed, idling away all the morning hours. When I closed my eyes, the sound of a knife being sharpened reached me. Uncle Hassan stashed the jackknife somewhere deep. I had no idea where he'd put it. His house had many secret corners. He could live hidden in this small house for at least thirty years without being detected.

A while ago, I was startled to see him jump out of the wall. I studied the wall later but couldn't see where he could have holed himself up. Uncle Amos pronounced that this was proof Uncle Hassan was turning into a ghost. He explained that anyone, whoever he was, would turn into a ghost when he was getting old. With this reasoning, Uncle Amos was old enough to have become a ghost many times over. When I mentioned it, he asked me whether he still looked like a human being. He sounded so serious that I didn't take it as a joke. I nodded. I said I was certain that he was human. He released a sigh of relief.

He stayed still for a minute but suddenly he fluttered his arms as if flapping wings. I thought he'd rather become a bird than a ghost. He said that the Greek sky was clearer and bluer than Korea's. According to him, Korea jutted out from a continent, too, but Greece pushed itself straight into the sea, so there was never a time when strong winds ceased to blow. Grapes and olives ripened in the wind and sometimes bells rang of their own accord in church belfries as if struck by angels.

To him, Korea was a godless land. When he first stepped onto Korean soil as a member of the dispatched army unit, he wept with his colleagues. I asked him why and he answered that it occurred to them that they probably couldn't leave this godless land alive. "Looking at American soldiers, we thought our premonition seemed all the more real. You may not know it, but a lot of soldiers from many countries were buried here. Not to mention Anglo-Saxons, who're the best performers at night—if they didn't have that remarkable ability, how could they have spread themselves all over the globe? Not a continent, not an ocean, hasn't been dirtied by them—there were Colombians, those lazy braggarts who used to spend their time drinking coffee in the Andes, the idiotic Thais who had stoves burning in their trenches and wouldn't budge when the temperature dipped ever so little, and the Filipinos, the guys we couldn't tell apart from the Thai bastards—Oh, God, please forgive me for mentioning those dirty pagans—the Dutch, who looked like they'd be only good to grow tulips in their gardens, and the French, who screeched like roosters and didn't look like men at all, and the cowardly Belgians, who looked over their shoulders to see what the French and the Dutch were doing, and the Luxemburg guys, who came with toy-like guns from their snot-sized country, and also there were stubborn Ethiopians, who thought night was morning, just like Jews . . . Who else? Yes, God! There were dirty Turks who reeked of nasty hookah and cinnamon whenever they opened their mouths. The guys who'd been doing nothing but pissing into the Bosporus Strait came in huge numbers, calling themselves men. If we hadn't been in Korea, we'd have aimed our guns at the Turks the first thing. When we Greeks kick the Turks' asses on Crete, they fly over the Aegean Sea and fall headlong in Cappadocia."

At this point, I felt I'd better bring him back to reality. If I let him drone on, he'd forget what he had set out to talk about and keep cursing Turkey and Uncle Hassan.

"Why did you come to a godless land?"

"Goddammit! I told you, didn't I?"

"You did. You sent an entire family to hell."

"Whenever you open your mouth, you reek of Hell's sulphuric fire . . . I didn't care at first. Where I was going, whatever I'd find there, I didn't mind as long as I could get out of my hometown, my motherland. I was young then. When I was leaving Piraeus Port—God bless that beautiful port!—on an American cargo ship, I felt I was going into God's bosom. I was one of the toiling people who'd put down his burden—I believed so. What else could I do? We were onboard for almost a month. Boring days. We learned simple Korean expressions and checked on our weapons. We had some jesters among us, so we had good laughs on the way. We are a people who can banter about life even in the middle of a vast sea. With the divine protection of Poseidon, we arrived safely at Busan Port. And when I stepped off the ship and set foot on this land, I was suddenly seized with homesickness and fear. It couldn't have been a feeling I had because I'm Greek. All the soldiers who came to this country, mobilized for other people's war, might have felt the same. By the way, who'd have thought we had to fight next to the Turks, our eternal enemy? We'd have been happy to reenact the Battle of Navarino with them any time, you see?"

After he said this, he turned his head to gaze far into the distance, as if in the direction of Greece. Would it have been different for Uncle Hassan? Everyone who'd traveled far to this land would have felt the same. Uncle Amos' eyes seemed to say so.

I, too, was one of those who arrived at an unfamiliar place after traveling a long road. If there was a difference for me, I didn't know where I came from. If I wasn't born from an egg, as legend had it for the progenitor of the Bak clan, I must have stayed for nine months in someone's womb and sucked her milk as a swaddled baby. I must have seen the sky of the same color as I was seeing now, and I must have breathed in the damp, polluted air, just like I was doing now. I must have babbled just like the babies in the neighborhood, and acquired the vocabulary of the language I was using now. If the right thing for me was to guess at these things, rather than remembering them, I'd be able to keep at it forever.

Uncle Amos said, "But, you know, somehow I felt I'd meet God here."

After lunch hours, customers ebbed out of the Chungnam Restaurant. Only then did Aunt Anna lay out food for us. My queasiness had subsided. I didn't find the smell of meat permeating the place intolerable. Yet, I couldn't bring myself to sip the sausage soup. Aunt Anna set for me a pot of soybean stew, boiled with potatoes, zucchini, mushrooms, green peppers, and tofu.

I could see the drunkard locksmith waking up from his nap. Two black sedans stopped in front of the grocery. Four women wearing dresses in vivid colors stepped out. The balding man we nicknamed Agent—shortened from real estate agent—guided them up the alley. Uncle Amos had quipped that Agent carried a mirror on his head. When he bowed his head, the round bald spot gave off light like a hand mirror.

After our table was cleared away and when Uncle Amos was drinking coffee, the women climbed down the hill and got into their cars. Aunt Anna muttered something I couldn't catch. She was probably lamenting her life.

I asked Uncle Amos, "So you met God? I want to meet Him, too. But why is it so hard to meet Him?"

He smiled. "It's not just God. There're so many guys who are hard to meet in this world. It's as if we live in a different world. If one of those rich ladies over there smiles in your direction, she isn't smiling at you. She's satisfied, realizing what a happy person she is, looking at a pathetic guy who lives a different life from hers."

Aunt Anna seemed pleased with his comment. "When I was

living with my in-laws, I offered the gods a bowl of clean water in the kitchen every day, but I'd never seen the Kitchen God, not even the tip of his nose. I've been to Buddhist temples hundreds of times, but I've never seen the heels of a real Buddha other than the heels of Buddha statues. If I were a god, I wouldn't appear for someone like you. If I appeared once, you'd spread the news high and low, and then all sorts of people would call me. Gods are busy as it is without a commotion like that, you see? One thing that's clear is this: The ladies over there and the Chungnam Restaurant cook are equal before God."

As always, everyone grew subdued after uttering and hearing a self-comforting remark like that. Aunt Anna, too, didn't seem to be convinced by her own words. The residents here were well aware that not all were equal before God. None of them doubted the maxim that they were equal before God when they were with their neighbors. The poor were jealous of each other but didn't hate each other from the bottom of their hearts. Someone in the neighborhood would have a lucky break once in a while. Then he slipped out, although it didn't happen often.

Yujong said that our neighborhood was a swamp on a hill. A swamp itself was nothing but a gigantic mouth. What was notable was that it didn't have an outlet. The swamp grew bigger and bigger with what it had swallowed. According to Yujong, no swamp was a swamp from the beginning. A swamp was formed when there was a large influx of soil and sand into a lake or when animal carcasses were piled up at the bottom.

"S . . . swamp is a part of a changing process. From a lake to a swa . . . swamp, from a swa . . . swamp to a ma . . . marsh . . . from a mar . . . marsh to a meadow . . . and when a pool is made in the me . . . meadow, it becomes a lake. If there's a di . . . difference, there's no cir . . . circulation."

Yujong said that after the swamp turned into a marsh, it was destined to become a desert.

He said that there was a passage in everyone's heart, through which a breeze went in and out. When a breeze went through a person's body, it took away moisture; and when it blew again, it brought moisture. That was how people didn't dry up as long as they were alive. I pictured the mute priest. He had said that we were all born from a tunnel. He said that a mother's womb was the coziest, the saddest, and the most shameless tunnel in the world. The same could be said about our neighborhood. People inched up from the level ground to the peak of the hill, expanding their residential zone. They made roads, put down utility poles, brought running water, and planted flowers. And now they could never go back to a time when there had been nothing, when the area had been a denuded hill. I thought I could vaguely grasp the meaning of the priest's tunnel. The tunnel pictured by the priest allowed only a one-way passage. It had to be a narrow passage in which you couldn't turn around and go back. Just as we couldn't crawl back into our mothers' wombs, the priest thought that the world was a narrow passage.

I tore off and chewed away the boring afternoon as if it were stale bread. When the muezzin's call to prayer stopped, Baldy and Smart-aleck returned from their excursion. Baldy looked stupefied just like a tank crewman who'd been hit by antitank bombs, whereas Smart-aleck had an expression that could be worn only by someone who was sick and tired of a boring joke, something like when the hill conquered after risking your life turns out to belong to your own forces.

I approached the drunkard and asked, "Who are they?"

"Elephants."

"What kind of elephants?"

"Pink elephants."

"What are they doing?"

"Passing by."

"Where are they headed?"

He didn't say anything.

I turned my head to gaze at the Chungnam Restaurant. Its

interior was clearly visible. It was crowded with customers. But the restaurant, filled with laughing and talking people, looked desolate. Even though so many people were merrily drinking and talking, it exuded sadness. A desert might look like this. If we went to a desert, all of us would turn into grains of sand. We were supposed to be broken into tiny pieces, scatter around, and seep into a throng of people. We would endure the long, hot day and the cold, never-ending night in the comfort of the rustles made by ever-desolate grains of sand brushing against each other. Then we would break into smaller fragments until we disappeared without a trace. If that was a desert, Yujong was right. This neighborhood was a swamp that would turn into a desert some day.

9

Smart-aleck's expression returned to what he'd worn when I first met him. Yujong and I sat quietly at the doorway, watching Smart-aleck practice putting on different expressions; sad, happy, and all sorts of other emotions. Uncle Hassan was nowhere in sight. I believed he was ensconced somewhere in the house.

The imam appeared, walking like a ghost. His shadow seemed to have shortened. Why was his shadow shorter even when the sun wasn't directly above us? It might indicate that the sunlight was piercing through his body. The penetration was partial now, but eventually all sunrays might go right through him.

Yujong cleared his throat and Smart-aleck, thinking that Yujong had spoken to him, started talking about what had happened the day before. We were hoping for just that but his storytelling was boring as usual.

Baldy and Smart-aleck, in soldierly precision, marched toward a gathering of brave war veterans. These two comrades-in-arms hadn't been in a battle together, but they got along fabulously; they commented on all the women they came across on the way. Smart-aleck, still harboring a fierce hatred of the rice store's second daughter, could bark like a dog at all the women.

The two were noun-like characters, so when they walked side by side, they became something of a compound noun. Baldy's mannerisms would come from Smart-aleck, and Smart-aleck's temperament would exude from Baldy. So they pounded the pavement as a compound noun, a totally different existence from their former selves.

Smart-aleck, with Baldy's field cap on, felt an unfathomable courage stirring in his heart. If someone had handed him a pole at the time, he could have used it to easily soar high and clear the roof of the South Gate. They arrived at their destination while keeping each other in check and cooperating with each other, just like two male dogs in rut.

Their destination was a big playing field. Smart-aleck's eyes bulged at the sight of the charter buses that had arrived from all over the country. These buses vomited out between thirty and fifty people each. The veterans, more energetic than reinforcement soldiers dispatched to the front, swarmed like maggots. For the first time in his life, Smart-aleck was simmering with a quiet thrill.

The veterans from other regions must have risen at the crack of dawn to make frantic preparations, but as they stepped down from the buses their faces looked refreshed as if they were just emerging from a sauna. They looked as determined as fathers pursuing their aberrant daughters, as furious as debt collectors demanding their money back. Smart-aleck said, "I was so intimidated that I felt I should say I came from a region, too, not from Seoul."

Baldy was all excitement. "All these guys are my comrades-in-arms." As if proving this statement, he shook hands and exchanged greetings with a lot of people, and inquired after their health. Smart-aleck had never seen him laugh and talk in such high spirits. He realized soon, however, that everyone gathered there offered greetings and inquired after each other, just as

Baldy had done.

The veterans sat in small clusters here and there, pouring liquor for each other and recounting their bygone exploits. Wherever the duo went, everyone talked about the same things. Smart-aleck lost interest bit by bit. He felt like he was watching a movie that consisted of battles from the beginning to the end. The talk of bayonets came from all directions; Hill 271, Hill 423, Hill 309, and Hill 188 were conquered and re-conquered innumerable times; and the sounds of mortars and bullets didn't stop.

Smart-aleck looked around. The trees encircling the field, as if guarding it, looked sinister, giving the impression of human forearms cut off at the elbows, with tree-tops resembling hands. Exhaust fumes coming from the engine-idling charter buses crawled among the people, making Smart-aleck's throat and eyes smart. Many people climbed up and down the podium to give speeches in the same intonation, but none paid any attention to them. Yet, the veterans ceaselessly clapped, nodded in agreement, spat out curses, and sang military songs.

By then, Smart-aleck was irritated. He expressed discontent to Baldy. "Dammit. Where're the real soldiers?" Baldy widened his eyes and said, "You can see them only on Soldiers' Day."

The veterans moved in ranks, too, all right, but they were not dignified soldiers in a parade, a far cry from Smart-aleck's expectations. They were not soldiers whose intelligent eyes sparkled behind dark sunglasses, with light refracting off their epaulets and belt buckles. Some gestured with hooks in lieu of hands, and others hobbled around, wielding their canes. A few had half of their faces gone, and many were missing an arm or a leg. At close range, their faded uniforms had fuzz balls and worn-out parts. A missed button or two was the order of the day and their boots were wrinkled. The heels that had come off their boots rolled around. Traces of dried kimchi juice were around the veterans' mouths, while gobbets of gummy matter, like abscesses, were caked at the corners of their eyes.

Baldy squeezed himself into groups of veterans and discussed battles with them. It seemed that no battle had been fought without his involvement. No battle was beyond his knowledge: Not to mention the early battles—Uijeongbu, Miari, the Han River defense battle, the Daejon street battle, and the Geum River defense battle—he was knowledgeable about the battles at the Naktong River defense line, the battles toward the end of the war, and the fierce battles to seize heights, which continued until the final days of war. Baldy waged an assault as a rifleman of the army, but soon he became an engineer soldier to carry out a river-crossing operation, and then he participated in a landing operation as a marine before transforming himself into a mortar shooter in a street battle. When veterans said something incorrect, Baldy promptly pointed it out and straightened them out. The veterans admired his memory and couldn't help being impressed that he remembered certain facts they hadn't been aware of despite their direct involvement in the particular battle, such as the operation plan, command documents, combat reports, detailed battle circumstances, quantity of the spoils, and even the number of casualties.

Meanwhile, speeches on the podium continued. Their theme was consistent: It is time for us, once again, to rescue this country that we have defended with our own lives; Let us punish the Reds, our enemy within. The speakers couldn't have sounded more confident; they seemed to be ready to rush out to eradicate the enemy if guns were pressed into their hands right then and there.

To Smart-aleck, however, they looked no better than stragglers. Their ruddy faces, with bulging veins, had spidery wrinkles, giving the impression that someone had scribbled on them, while the leathery skin of their necks, with walnut-sized Adam's Apples protruding in the middle, reminded him of plucked chickens. Some big-bellied veterans were good-looking, but some had a child's gait while others, though tall and skinny, had severely bent backs, making their entire bodies tremble when they tried to gaze straight ahead. If they put their finger on a trigger, the tremor in their hand would certainly make them fire at anyone, friend or foe, and their shoulders seemed too narrow to sling any military equipment over.

The scenes and soldiers imagined by Smart-aleck were nowhere in evidence, even though he rubbed his eyes for a better look. It was Baldy who had told him that the brave soldiers would be in a disciplined parade and many flags would fly dazzlingly in the wind. But the place seemed to be a venue for cranky oldsters, who had been plucked out of senior centers all over the country to compete over who'd been most unfairly treated by life.

Baldy didn't decline any drink offered by the veterans and ate their food more heartily than ever before. Smart-aleck also had pastry and milk handed over by a veteran, who had only two fingernails remaining on his hand. The boy felt as if he were chewing and drinking nails. His stomach felt queasy. Squatting between buses, he threw up. Sour gastric juices left a bitter aftertaste in his mouth. A one-armed veteran gave him some water. The water tasted like a human arm.

Smart-aleck weaved through the crowd to look for Baldy. A short, sturdy veteran, with half of his head caved in, was grabbing Baldy by the throat and bullying him. The two men had gotten in an argument while exchanging their exploits, each claiming that his own memory was right. The veteran demanded that Baldy reveal his rank and name. Baldy told him the unit and the affiliation he'd served in. The veteran let go of Baldy's collar. "Ha, you're that notorious Fake Soldier." Other veterans talked among themselves in low voices. The throat-grabber said, "No wonder he knows more than I do." Someone else said, "We've got to teach a bastard like him a lesson. A bastard who wasn't a soldier acts like a war veteran and sullies our honor." A veteran slapped Baldy across the cheek. Smart-aleck kicked this veteran in the crotch. Smart-aleck was slapped, too. But the veterans soon lost interest in the duo. Smart-aleck found his way out of the crowd, fuming in anger.

The duo, once a compound noun, split themselves to return to their own proper-noun status. On the way home, Smart-aleck asked Baldy, "Did you lie to me?"

Baldy stubbornly shook his head.

"Then what did they mean by Fake Soldier?"

Baldy grew sullen but didn't say anything. Smart-aleck threw a punch at Baldy's chest. As a result, a medal fell off. Baldy bent down to pick it up. The medal could be a fake, too, one that he himself had made. With this thought, Smart-aleck felt as if he'd been more unfairly treated by life than all the veterans out there in the field had been. But his fury didn't last long. Fast surrender was his strong suit.

"Who cares? I'm going to die."

Baldy blanched and made excuses but nothing reached Smart-aleck's ears. The rest was history. They returned to our rundown neighborhood as I'd described before: Baldy looking stupefied just like a tank crewman who'd been hit by antitank bombs and Smart-aleck with an expression that could be worn only by someone who was sick and tired of a boring joke, something like the hill conquered by risking your life turning out to belong to your own forces. They returned with no battle results or war spoils to show for their outing.

Early in the morning, I went to the park with Uncle Hassan. After he suspended his business, he often went there without me. He'd be off somewhere but returned at prayer time without fail. He didn't encourage me to pray with him. He didn't say that my watching him disturbed his prayers, either. He knew how to pray naturally, just like eating or breathing.

Once, the proselytizer opened his Bible on our table and boasted about the breadth of his knowledge, scrolling his finger down the passages he was reciting. It looked like his sense of verbal competition had been fired up by the imam, who was sitting on Smart-aleck's bench, blankly looking down at the city. His eyes closed, the proselytizer moved his finger to prove how profoundly he understood the Bible and how deeply the passages were engraved in his heart. Then he asked the imam to talk about the Koran, adding a precondition: If there's something in the Koran that's worthwhile to listen to, that is.

The imam shook his head. The proselytizer put on a meaningful smile. The imam shook his head again. He pointed to Uncle Hassan and said, "There's no fixed meaning in the Koran. Depending on who accepts it, it can become holy words or evil temptations. If you still feel you must hear a passage from the Koran, ask him. As far as I know, Hassan is the only Hafiz who can recite the Koran forward and backward." Only then did I understand why there was no copy of the Koran, revered by Muslims as a divine gift, in the house. The imam's seemingly casual comment threw the proselytizer off. The corners of his eyes fluttered. His cheeks grew taut, accentuating his high cheekbones, and a deep sigh escaped between his thin lips. The proselytizer slammed his Bible shut, tucked it under his arm, and backed away. From his cautious but comical backward steps, I sensed respect and decorum. The feeling must have been mutual for Uncle Hassan. Unlike other times, he followed him to the doorway and saw him off.

When he prayed, Uncle Hassan mumbled in his mother tongue—if not, in Arabic, the language of the Koran—so I couldn't make heads or tails of it. But just as I could be moved by music without knowing which instrument was playing it, I loved his rumbling voice, which conveyed much more tranquility and subdued passion than the muezzin's.

The park in the early morning hours couldn't be further from a refreshing oasis. Trash flew about, canceling out fresh fragrances rising from dew-covered plants and damp soil, and homeless people soaked in dew lay around like discarded newspapers. Some of them looked familiar. Uncle Hassan stared at a man for a long time. I recognized him, too. The curly-haired young man.

I'd seen him being taunted by his group. He would walk with

his narrow shoulders hunched, giving the impression of a pet imported from some foreign land. The sleeping people, feeling our footsteps, opened their eyes but immediately shut them. The curly-haired man blinked his eyes and bolted upright. He looked around. He seemed to be wondering why he'd been sleeping there. He pressed his temples with his fingers for a while, glanced in our direction, and slowly walked to the public toilet. The back of his hair was squashed in swirls, giving the impression that a worn-out coil of mesh scouring pad was bobbing up and down above his shoulders. From the back, as if aged decades overnight, he looked like an old man whose days were numbered. He turned his head to look back at us. His eyes locked briefly with mine, as his tongue flickered around his lips. As if to offer an excuse, he opened his arms and shrugged his shoulders. From his eyes and gesture, I sensed a vague longing. He seemed envious of me and Uncle Hassan. He wouldn't have felt the same way if he'd seen my scars. He wouldn't have felt the same way if he'd seen Uncle Hassan cutting up a chunk of pork amid his customers' insulting remarks. I couldn't be sure, of course. At times, everything, except oneself, could be an object of longing and envy.

Right before I left the orphanage trailing Uncle Hassan, I made a quick mental inventory of my possessions. I didn't have any attachment to any single item of what had been given to me temporarily. If I could, I would have taken off what I was wearing and followed him out naked.

I always dreamed of taking a break from my life without giving notice. I had no idea whether Uncle Hassan would give me the opportunity, but I knew that such a break could come suddenly. If I'd been asked what I'd do during my break, I would have answered that I'd do something unimportant, like sleeping all day long in a place where no one was around or reading my favorite book without being disturbed.

Unimportant things were important to me. I simply wanted to escape from trivial things, like walking to the cafeteria in line holding our sectional meal trays, using our utensils without clanking, or chewing kimchi with our mouths shut. Uncle Hassan's eyes asked me what I was thinking. I opened the bag the director had packed for me and took out only my notebook, where I'd collected faces. Tucking it under my arm as if it were my birth certificate, I followed him out. He didn't ask what I was carrying. I was grateful. Things that were precious to me but had no value to others, things that would embarrass me when others found out what it was as though it were my dirty underwear—my scrapbook was one of such things. To tell the truth, at the time I longed for everything except myself and my scrapbook.

I realized at the moment that everything, save for what I owned, would remain an object of longing.

Returning from the park, we stopped by at the Chungnam Restaurant. Aunt Anna said that her head ached because Baldy had sung military songs mournfully the night before. "After a while, my heart started pounding. I felt as if a cicada was clinging to my heart. Where else do you find a person who sings military songs as achingly as the singer Bae Ho? I should leave this neighborhood. This is too much, too freaky."

Aunt Anna trotted out twenty proverbs or so that lamented a wretched lot in life before disappearing through the kitchen's back door. Uncle Hassan returned home and I turned newspaper pages to look for faces I hadn't cut out yet. I'd owned only one scrapbook when I left the orphanage but now I had four. I kept the first three at home and the fourth at the restaurant. No face was the same in my collection, but whenever I leafed through newspapers and magazines searching for new faces, I found the same faces that contained all the expressions human faces could wear.

Aunt Anna approached me, wiping her hands on her apron. Peeking at my notebook, she cocked her head. "It's strange. Why isn't there a happy face? Look. Look at the faces you've collected. Don't you think it's strange? Even smiling faces look sad somehow."

I wanted to reply that the expressions were read differently from viewer to viewer.

She went on, "That old Turk is to blame. What did he do, making a child select all these stupefied faces?" She slipped a smile.

I was almost tricked by her. I thought I'd love to put her face into the scrapbook right then, with her wry, lovely expression.

She said, "What's the use of saying it? The guy called Happiness is blind where we are. He knows how to touch the faces of some undeserving guys. He never visits people like us."

As I approached home, the air was heavy with the smell of Turkish meatballs Uncle Hassan was making. Smart-aleck was lying flat on the bench looking up at the sky. I lay next to him in the same posture and looked up at the sky as he did. The human gaze had no limit. We could look anywhere. I knew that over the sky was outer space. I also knew that the sky was part of that outer space. So, the moment I looked at the sky, my gaze was already running toward the endless space. But I couldn't see my fate when I put my palm close to my eyes to study the fate lines there, and I couldn't see my fate when I looked at the boundless sky. That is what the human gaze is for, I thought. The things we couldn't see even if we looked and the things we had to look at even if we couldn't see—these were all contained in the human gaze.

"I couldn't sleep a wink last night," Smart-aleck mumbled, "You heard it too. The songs Baldy was singing, right?" His face was as sallow as lemon rind.

I'd heard him, and Uncle Hassan had heard him, too. It was possible all our neighbors had heard him. Uncle Hassan had moaned as if paralyzed in a nightmare. Baldy's voice had a haunting ring. It pierced our ears with a heavy, persistent ring, just like the sound of a hammer echoing through a long, dilapidated drain pipe. Then it finally wrapped around us like a cape and tightly reined us in. We met dawn with our bodies bound up by the sound of his songs. A bluish hue spread in the room as day was about to break. Until then, Baldy didn't stop singing.

People in ancient times believed that music we couldn't hear was being played constantly in outer space. If they imagined that, how much they must have wanted to hear the motions of stars and the movements of the celestial sphere! If such music existed in outer space, it would be similar to Baldy's song, I thought. The sounds made by all living things to prove their existence had a sad ring to them. The loud bang at the moment of the universe's creation could have been only a negligible soft noise. Music is perceived as music, not by the intensity of its pitch, but by how it strikes a chord in our soul.

Standing at the bottom of the stairs near his home, Baldy looked in our direction. The yellow-striped cat rubbed herself against his leg. A black plastic bag dangled from his fingers. Smart-aleck turned his head, and upon catching sight of Baldy, he jumped up, picked up a chestnut-sized stone lying under his bench, and heaved it at him. The stone fell impotently at Baldy's feet. The hair on the cat's tail and the rest of her body bristled.

"Go away! Go!" Smart-aleck shouted.

It looked like a scene in a third-rate melodrama. Baldy tossed the black plastic bag toward us. With gloomy eyes, Smart-aleck looked down at the bag that had landed in front of the bench. The cat frisked over and sniffed at it. Baldy turned around as stiffly as a compass and walked away, leaning into the empty air, as if he were supporting himself with an invisible cane.

Smart-aleck explained: "Uncle Baldy can't remember, he says. From the day the war broke out to the day of the ceasefire. His memory of those three years was erased. Records show that he was buried in a trench and then rescued. What he had is called post-traumatic stress disorder. People experience again and again the horrible things they went through. When it's deemed too hard to endure, the brain wipes out everything. So for him, all the years were reversed to the time when the war broke out.

Other memories are useless. They've become meaningless because the gap in the middle isn't filled up. We're more easily tempted by what we don't remember than what we remember. From the moment he realized there was a hole in his memory, he started studying. He wanted to recover the years he'd lost. He memorized down to the number of bullets fired in a battle. But he could never revive his memory no matter how many details he looked up about a battle he thought he'd been part of . . . Do you remember the day before yesterday? I was here frowning at you, right? Actually, I couldn't remember your name, so that's why I was frowning. Of course, your name came to me later. You rack your brain to remember a name and your head hurts so much. What can be comparable to the pain he feels, the man who's lost three years of his youth? I've been thinking about that. I believed war was terrible but at the same time it was beautiful and sublime as in the movies. How did I get to have an obscene belief like that? Who taught me all the things that I believe to be right at this moment? Do you think that's what life is all about?"

Uncle Hassan brought out Turkish meatballs for us. Smart-aleck didn't touch them. Instead, he picked up the black plastic bag and took out a cookie from it. He hugged the cat and tried to feed her the cookie from Baldy's care package. The cat licked it a few times but soon lost interest and fell asleep in his arms.

Uncle Hassan stroked Smart-aleck on the head and said, "Don't hate him so much. Don't be so upset even if he exaggerated his specialty and he prettied himself up for you. He is a person whose soul was hurt. He'd have chosen to defend his soul, if he could have done it by giving up an arm or a leg. If there're people we should trust, he's one of them."

I wanted to ask Uncle Hassan. What were my scars supposed to defend? Did I have the soul to defend in the first place? If so, why was my soul still poverty-stricken? Why did both my body and soul get hurt? My soul couldn't defend my body and my body couldn't defend my soul; then, did it mean that my soul and my body had never been one?

Smart-aleck built a jungle gym in his head and started exploring it. Once in a while, he asked Yujong and me if we could contribute. He explained about the path he'd found and cautiously asked if it sounded practicable. The operation that unfolded in his head was far from good. For one thing, there was almost no case in which a mentally ill person had been recognized for his distinguished service to the state. Proving that someone had suffered from PTSD wasn't easier. Nothing seemed easy, from finding a lawyer who'd take on the case to devising ways to come up with the expenses. Smart-aleck entertained the idea of becoming a masked burglar. But by his own calculation, obtaining the expenses through masked burglary would take seventy years. Even if he had been determined to fulfill his mission in his son's generation, it would be useless. Baldy, by then, would be in his grave.

"This is a matter of honor. I will do everything in my power to recover his honor."Smart-aleck was afraid of older people. "I sense something odd from older people. Especially people who've been rich for a long time seem to have a cruel streak. How many people did they exploit to live affluently for so long in a place where most people scrape by day to day? The veterans I met might be cruel, too. They survived the war, didn't they? But I wasn't afraid of them. They spewed sharp words and wore tough expressions, but I wasn't afraid of them. I only sensed their blind fury. That kind of fury tends to be directed to themselves. Uncle Baldy is barely hanging in there with his singing. Otherwise, he'd have broken into pieces and disappeared."

Smart-aleck talked about a desert, too. Love grows on a desert, too. "People brushed away the veterans as fools. Uncle Baldy is like a man who's just found out the woman he loved is actually a man. That's why people are making fun of him. But think: What if the person I loved isn't a woman? Is it a crime if she turned out to be a man? Nothing is more important—even if he turns out to be a monster, not human—than the fact that you loved the person. But people are making fun of the veterans, saying that they're fools and idiots. They belittle the veterans and look down on them, asking why they didn't know there was no fatherland to defend in the first place. The veterans were taken advantage of and then thrown out. They know it, too. But there's nothing else they can do. That is the truth."

Yujong backed up Smart-aleck's theory. "The s . . . same words don't me . . . mean they . . . they're the same. Whatever the veterans say, they may be simp . . . simply say . . . saying . . . they're hung . . . hungry."

Aunt Anna said she didn't remember the war. Not because she'd contracted a disease like Baldy but because she'd been too young: "Wasn't I lucky? If I remembered the war in addition to what I'd been through, I'd have gone crazy a long time ago. There're so many things that are better forgotten. The war? Just thinking about it is horrible . . . There's a story I heard. It's about my cousin. She had one baby after another before the war, but she couldn't during the war. After the war, she was pregnant again like magic! If what I think is right, the old man Baldy either doesn't know the war is over or he's pretending he doesn't know it. If he accepts that the war is over, his memory may come back, just like my cousin who got pregnant again."

I thought Aunt Anna could be right. Then how unfamiliar and frightening Baldy must have been to himself all these years? In the future, how would Baldy remember himself, who was dressed in military uniform and sang military songs he didn't quite know, dragged by a habit, who was startled by his own reflection in the mirror and flustered by the songs he sang while enduring decades of breathing and eating, controlled by the memories imprinted in his body? With no one telling him for how long he was supposed to live like that, all the fear he'd felt had been solely his. Uncle Amos went to see Baldy to hear all about the Greek army in Korea. After learning from Baldy what he hadn't known before, Uncle

Amos broke down and cried for a long time.

Then he asked, "What was our Greek army like? Please be frank with me."

Baldy pronounced with conviction, "They couldn't have been braver. The Greek soldiers knew what justice was. As far as I remember, they committed no misdeed on this land. They were as wise as the Athenian army and as brave as the Spartan army. They didn't take anything from this land; rather, they made it fertile with their flesh and blood. They were noble foreigners who came here to sacrifice themselves. Following the command of the God they worshiped."

Uncle Amos's trembling hands grabbed Baldy's dry hands. He squeezed out the words with much effort, "Than . . . Thank you. Thank you very much."

If I were ever asked to list embarrassing scenes, I'd promptly put this scene high on the list: two old men weeping, clasping each other's hands. The two veterans exchanged with their eyes what words failed to convey. Although they hadn't run into each other on the battlefield, it was clear that they had a lot to talk about. I had nothing to say. Having things to say meant you had a past. I had no one who shared my past. No one knew about my origins and I didn't, either. It was as if I were standing in the middle of a road in a blizzard. Nowhere could I find my footprints except where I stood. Even my footprints at this very moment couldn't be seen, concealed under my own feet. As soon as I took a step to examine them, they would be erased. I was an existence that went forward, sealing its past. Whether I wanted it or not, I had no choice but to move toward the future. I'd never been so pained about the word "future." A premonition grew like a tumor; perhaps the future permitted to me would turn out to be a desert.

I pulled down my three scrapbooks from the shelf and put them on the desk. A waft of subtle fragrance drifted out as I opened a scrapbook. A human fragrance mixed with the smells of the old paper and ink. I could sympathize with tribes who believed that their soul would be stolen if they had their photo taken.

Uncle Amos, too, said something similar. In the winter of 1951, he had witnessed an illegal execution for the first time since his participation in the Korean War. As if in ancient times—war always takes people back to ancient times—a man's neck was chopped off with a big sword. He saw an annual ring on the sliced section of the neck. This was when he began to have the belief that people leave behind the markings of their lives in one way or another.

"That was when I knew for the first time that people's bodies have an annual ring. I didn't believe things like that in the beginning. I thought that Koreans who said things like that were barbarians. But after I witnessed what I did, there was no way I could refuse to believe it. That was an issue that constantly bothered me. You know, people torment themselves all their lives over some useless issue, not over their daily bread."

Sometimes I had an urge to chop off my finger to check on its section. If I found an annual ring, I'd at least know how long I'd resided in this world. But I couldn't muster up the courage to cut off a mere finger, not an arm, not a leg, not the neck. So one thing became obvious. That my scars hadn't been self-inflicted. I wouldn't have had the strength to do that as a small child, and after I'd gained enough strength, I didn't have the courage.

I studied every face in my collection. Some were handsome and some ugly. More, however, looked ordinary, making it hard to judge whether they were good-looking or not. Being ordinary was ambiguous, too. Passing judgment wasn't as easy as I'd first thought. A good-looking face looked the opposite the next time I checked.

Uncle Hassan dozed, resting his feet on the table. I alternated my gaze between the thick soles of Uncle Hassan's feet and the faces I'd put in the scrapbook. His soles had an expression, too. I'd describe it as an expression you'd wear when you start chewing crushed ginger thinking it was mashed potato.

Half awake, Uncle Hassan asked, "What are you going to do with those photos?"

"I'm not sure. Maybe I'll keep collecting faces forever like this."

"Don't be disappointed even if you don't find a familiar face. You may not find a face that jolts your memory, but your memory is entirely yours. No need to rely on photos."

"It's not that. I don't expect anything."

"I see that one thing is missing. You're collecting all kinds of expressions worn by countless people. But you shouldn't forget that a single person can wear thousands of expressions."

I was offended. I put my scrapbooks back on the shelf and went over to the Chungnam Restaurant. Uncle Hassan must have been referring to the fact that I'd cried in his arms calling out to Mom. I'd stressed many times: I wasn't calling Mom. It wasn't me who cried like that. Just another me who'd been hiding inside me. It was another me, whom I'd encountered throughout my life a few times at most.

The restaurant still exuded loneliness. Yujong's father, the coal briquette seller, and the rice seller Kim, the walking dictionary of swear words, grabbed each other by the collar, but no one raised their eyebrows. Grappling was part of the landscape in the restaurant. It was something like a scene in a movie other diners watched while chomping on small radish kimchi and fresh green peppers in lieu of popcorn. As always, the walking dictionary of swear words was defeated. No swear words could defeat the vernacular. Swear words could win only tentatively.

Kim could be a winner while invoking all the dogs in the world, dog this, dog that, dog here, dog there. All Yujong's father did was to hear him out before asking, "You sure you're human?" Then Kim had to wonder whether he was really human even after he went home. He could invite sleep under the influence of alcohol, but he'd surely open his eyes at dawn. "Did he mean I'm not human?" He'd scream at times, and recovering his calm he'd ask himself whether he was human. This question would burst upon him and harass him as he weighed rice on a scale, as he put on his shoes, and as he slapped his second daughter on the cheek. To comfort himself, he'd create more swear words, and the more he did, the bigger bundle of doubts he would get in return. He'd feel wronged, wondering why he was getting more insult than he'd given, but he persistently tossed out swear words without the slightest doubt of his victory. And he was admonished by the coal briquette seller all the time.

What rules our life is the vernacular, not swear words. The world is made in such a way that simple language wins: money, love, honor, friendship, happiness... The world ruled by ordinary words is calm but boring. There, swear words are useless. Numerous offensive words flying around in the restaurant grew trite and were tamed into idiomatic expressions. Even swear words were trapped by the vernacular, gradually losing their sharp edges and vulgarity before being integrated into it. When all was said and done, the result of the fight between Kim and the briquette seller was predetermined. Yet, there wasn't a single victor in the restaurant. Because all were timid. The characteristic of the timid was that they were sensitive to being criticized. In other words, by definition, people who could let criticism go in one ear and out the other were broad-minded. The diners couldn't stand it if they were misunderstood. If they heard their names mentioned, their ears pricked up while their eyes were nonchalantly fixed on the street outside the glass door.

A broad-minded person was sitting in a corner of the restaurant. He was an old man around Uncle Hassan's age. His unkempt gray beard was soggy with alcohol and his fingers gripping a cup were gnarled. Deep furrows were etched over his thick eyebrows, as if a triangular chisel had gone over it, and his complexion was dark like a crop afflicted with anthracnose. He gave off the impression of the solid surface of quartz from the short bristle of gray hair and the shape of his pursed lips, with corners turned down in right angles like a door knocker. His eyes didn't roam at all. He was quiet and intent. He looked like a person who knew how to effectively conceal his inborn dullness. The only vacant seat was across from him. Taking the seat, I looked around at all the drinkers. The duo who'd been at each other's throats had resumed being drinking buddies, as if nothing had happened. Actually, in this restaurant, if a person went out briefly, his seat cast a looming presence. If someone went to the toilet, others kept silent, and were flustered by their own silence. When the person returned, a buzz rose up once again. No one, for this reason, was sent away from the restaurant against his will. The old man looked up to glance at me as I sat down, and that was all—otherwise, he didn't look around at all. If there was a gaze turned inward, his gaze would be it.

Untypically, Aunt Anna wasn't drawn into any of her customers' conversations. With her mouth shut, she bustled around in the kitchen like a squirrel on a wheel. Her movements were busy but she looked precarious somehow. She dropped dishes more often than usual, and even the dishes rolling on the floor clanged more loudly.

I liked the peaceful bustle in the restaurant. No one was shabby here. It didn't matter if God didn't watch over you and it was okay if luck didn't come your way. If the devil had visited, you wouldn't be afraid, and if misfortune made a surprise attack, you wouldn't be frightened. The imam, blending in with the darkness, passed the front of the restaurant, and then Smart-aleck, in agony, passed by. The proselytizer passed by reciting the Bible, and Yujong pressed his face on the glass pane to peek inside before walking away. The drunkard locksmith came in to take out some liquor, and Baldy and Uncle Amos squatted in front of the restaurant for a while before moving on. Meanwhile, the moon shifted by a hand's width to the west, some stars disappeared and others appeared. The wind, blowing down from the school's animal cage, knocked on the door before moving on downward, and the moonlight refracting off the white body of the mosque was absorbed into the light of the street lamp in front of the restaurant. I could watch the world go around while sitting in the small dirty restaurant.

The night deepened. Aunt Anna drove out her customers earlier than usual. The drunken people scattered into the dark, chuckling and chortling. Only the old man in the corner remained. He stuck his finger in his cup to stir his liquor. The sour smell that had welled up in the restaurant had thinned. I helped Aunt Anna clean up. I turned the chairs upside down on the tables and swept the floor.

Aunt Anna addressed me, "Why aren't you moving your butt at this hour? You fought with the old Turk, right? You shouldn't fight with oldsters. Think how much they must've fought with how many people until they reached their age. So you, at least, shouldn't."

The ceiling shook. Uncle Amos was bustling about in his attic. Soon, his footsteps thumped down the stairs. He was going to put up the wooden shutter for Aunt Anna. She stole a glance at the old man in the corner. As if to show that it was his final cup, he threw back his head to drink it up and then wiped his mouth with the back of his hand. He rose and left the restaurant with a steady gait. Uncle Amos closed the door and closed the wooden shutter. The night was dark and lonesome. In this neighborhood, even night was steeped in poverty. Lit by the lamplight, the old man looked down at the side road for a while. Uncle Amos dusted off his hands and climbed up to his attic. The old man turned around to look in the direction of Aunt Anna and me. Bringing his gnarled hand to his mouth, he cleared his throat.

A thick voice drifted out of his mouth. "You, are you well?" Aunt Anna nodded ever so slightly.

"I'll make it short. He died. At the end of last month. He drank and went to the rice paddy, and slipped into the water sluice . . . I know you don't have any feelings left for him. Still, as his father, I thought I should tell you. Please forgive him now. Pray for his good rest, if not for his rebirth in a better world."

She didn't reply or nod.

He heaved a sigh. "My grandchildren are your children. Now that he's gone, there's nothing for you to be afraid of. Come any time if you want to see them . . . I'll take my leave now."

He awkwardly raised his right arm and then put it down.

As he was removing himself from the pool of lamplight, Aunt Anna spoke. "It's late. How'll you get home?"

"I'll close my eyes briefly at the station and then it'll be time for the first train. Don't you worry."

He blended into the darkness. Like stepping stones, he appeared from time to time under the lamps. Soon, he disappeared around the bend. Aunt Anna crumpled down in a heap. Aunt Anna, the queen of scars. The latent pain was trying to emerge using her scars as outlets. I knew the pain so well. That was how my scars, too, asserted their existence.

"Are you all right?"

The list of words we could offer to a person in pain was all too short. Compared with other abilities, we ruefully lack the ability to comfort others. Aunt Anna looked up with eyes full of moisture. She stretched out her chubby hand to pull down my arm. I kneeled and put my cheek on her abundant chest.

"I'm not all right. How can I be all right? To survive, adults should cry like children from time to time. I was going to hear the news and I was going to see him one of these days. I called him Father-in-Law once and he called me his daughter-in-law. I knew it would happen and I'm just experiencing what was destined to happen. Not that knowing doesn't make you unhurt. But . . . I'm worried more about you. You, too, probably before long, in the very near future, will have to confront your past. The pain you'll have to put up with, the memories you've buried deep in your heart, will untangle themselves and spread to every corner of your body like poison, hurting you, and that makes me weep . . . I love you, child."

Aunt Anna seemed to say that the past was the seismic center of the earthquake erupting in the human body. If we could peek into our interior by bisecting our chest, we would be able to discover the past crouching there. A strong quake at a magnitude of ten on the Richter scale passed through Aunt Anna. She pressed her eyes with her palms in an effort to get rid of swelling on her eyelids.

"It's too late. Go on in. The old Turk must be awake, rolling his heavy eyeballs, wondering if you ran away. If he knew I kept you this late, you know what evil eye he's going to give me in the morning, that gruff old man. He won't show me his eyebrow trick for a while." She pushed my back to urge me home.

The house was dark. I couldn't hear Uncle Hassan breathing. When I lay down next to him, he turned over, facing the wall. He tried hard to heave sighs without making any sound, but his thin, long breathing reached my ears clearly. Pretending that it was an accident, I draped my arm on his torso. I could feel his peaceful tremor. I soon fell asleep.

10

Closed for the Day: the phrase Aunt Anna came up with after racking her brain for an hour. I wrote it down on a piece of paper as instructed and put it up on the restaurant's glass door.

"What's this? You say you're closed with your doors wide open?" The road repairmen hired by the local government complained when they came in for breakfast but were turned away.

Aunt Anna retorted, "Is it okay if you loaf on the job and get paid for your so-called work?"

"Don't slander us. Who's loafing?"

"So why do you care if someone else isn't open for business with her doors open, or eats noodles after cooking rice?"

Watching her all morning, I wondered whether she declared the restaurant to be "closed" just so she could enjoy herself with smart comebacks like this for the customers who were coming in.

Aunt Anna said to me, "This is a hassle. Let's close up properly. Come here and help me."

Following her instructions, I pulled out all the chairs and gathered them in a corner and put together all the tables in the middle of the room. She took off her slippers and climbed on top of the tables, grunting, and lay on her side, like a mermaid. When someone entered, she silently sent him away with the flick of her wrist. With a hand cradling her head, she dozed off, breathing evenly like a sleeping child. Then I had to wave people away.

Uncle Amos knew what had happened the night before, so he didn't bother her; instead he rummaged through the kitchen for a bite. Then, he made an X with his arms and scratched his entire body. "I couldn't sleep a wink because of the mosquitoes. Burning repelling incense is useless. I might die of suffocation before the mosquitoes do. God is furious. He sent us vampires. Oh, God, do you really intend to siphon off our blood until we're dried up?"

He must have felt sheepish about adding a wish that God would grant us a stronger mosquito repellent. After scratching his arms and legs dotted with scabs, he started washing dishes. At the clattering sound, Aunt Anna's eyes opened wide. She slowly shut them again, probably realizing that she was enjoying her day off, a truly rare occasion. She'd briefly squirmed with the intention of getting up, opening a gap between the tables. Uncle Amos was about to leave the restaurant when he tripped on the threshold. He got up, rubbing his knee and calf, and glared at the threshold as if at an enemy.

"Dammit! Everything in the world is hostile to humans now. Before long, land will reject the growth of plants, animals will get back at us, and the earth will spit humans into outer space."

Uncle Amos would be the first human the earth would spit out. He had the knack of tickling people, so the earth wouldn't be able to hold in a sneeze.

The day passed calmly. Now the wretched woman was laid out on the tables, which used to hold earthenware bowls of blood sausage soup, dishes of cabbage kimchi and radish kimchi, lidded containers for salt and a seasoning mix, spoons and chopsticks, water glasses, liquor cups, and liquor bottles. Sleeping on the tables, like a sacrificial lamb dedicated to the restaurant, was the foolish woman who didn't know how to deal with her own pain, although she had the mysterious curative powers to heal the sick simply by stroking them a few times with her eyes, voice, and rough hands.

Her sleeping face was peculiar. She looked like a typical Korean woman but then it would be credible if someone said she was of Chinese, Japanese, Vietnamese, or Indonesian descent. She could have been a Hispanic, a mulatto, or a Native American with some black blood thrown in. In the end, I was confused about who she was, whose blood she inherited, and it began to dawn on me that people were born with mixed blood. It was the same with Uncle Hassan and Uncle Amos. They had spent so many years in Korea that despite their stubborn personalities, they'd been tamed by the place. Some recognized them as foreign on sight, but others didn't have a clue about their foreign origins. Some people, even after they were told that the duo was from Turkey and Greece, insisted that they had to be Korean. They offered what they called evidence, saying that the two men resembled so-and-so they knew and that so-and-so they knew was doubtlessly Korean, and therefore . . . The neighborhood residents rarely held a misconception like that, probably because they knew who Uncle Hassan and Uncle Amos were. As Aunt Anna said, knowing was not necessarily better than ignorance.

Aunt Anna turned over. The gap between the tables widened. She was dreaming. I bet it was a terrible dream. She moved her lips slightly but couldn't say anything in her sleep. Soon, big fat tears leaked out of her swollen eyelids. From time to time, I too shed tears in the middle of a dream. This woman—who'd weave through the tables, set out food, pour drinks, snub people, and count money—was now dreaming sprawled on the tables, like a gigantic bridge connecting them. She was sleeping as if she had been born there.

The faded sunlight sneaked into the restaurant like a cat, and bathed it. With squinted eyes, I looked out. The day was coming to a close. The day, one of the numerous days of my life, was ending. Aunt Anna, awake without my noticing it, was looking out the door, her eyes alert. The outside world was reflected intact in her pupils. I offered her what Uncle Hassan had taught me, a customary Turkish phrase: "I hope you had a nice dream."

When Aunt Anna spoke, she seemed unaware of my presence. "I was in my childhood home. It was an old thatched-roof house that didn't even have a fence. Still, flowers blossomed in the front yard and dogs frolicked. We had chickens and ducks. In the barn, we had oxen and pigs. In the back was a stand for sauce jars, and a big linden tree shadowed it like a sunshade. Next to the shed was a persimmon tree and across it was a big apricot tree. Beside the kitchen garden in front of our house was an overgrown paulownia that had leaves so big that they didn't rustle if an ordinary wind passed through. Under it was a short camellia. Seven of us grew up in that house. I had two older sisters and two older brothers, and I had a younger brother and a younger sister. My eldest sister was married off as a replacement for someone's dead wife in the next village but died of tuberculosis, and one of my elder brothers was involved in a crime, so he was sent to prison and didn't come out alive. Lives fell like camellia flowers. Grandfather, Grandmother, and Father died in that house. But the house didn't get old at all. It looked the same when I was small and when I was getting married. People were born, grew up, and got old in that house, but it didn't grow old or worn out, feeding on our family's blood, tears, and flesh. I was terrified by the house sometimes. I wanted to get out of that house and thought I'd never return once I left home. But you know what? The older I get, the more I miss that house. I went to visit my childhood home in my dream. I walked along the familiar village road, passed the houses of my old friends, and reached the kitchen garden next to the paulownia . . . but I found an empty lot with no trace of a house. I couldn't see the thatched roof, the roof that my grandfather and father used to weave themselves and put up every spring . . . I knew that my childhood had disappeared without a trace like that. In my dream, I wasn't flustered. I knew it'd turn out like that. Knew that it'd turn out like that in the end..."

Adults are people who are jealous of children, with a look that says children are fools who don't know what precious things they possess. Uncle Amos had told me that Aunt Anna had children. They didn't know that she was their mother, he said. If Aunt Anna wanted, I'd be happy to become her son. The scars on my body could be proof that I was her son. Mother and son were supposed to have similar scars, weren't they? As Aunt Anna climbed down from the tables, she tumbled to the floor. The tables had shifted away from each other, creating a gulf in between. She wasn't hurt, though. In her restaurant, not a hair of hers would be hurt, even if her opponent was the legendary general Yi Sunsin. After cursing the tables and gravity a few times, she reverted to her normal self. Several passersby noticed her standing in the kitchen and came in, thinking she'd opened for business.

"Do you guys keep your eyes in your pockets, like candies? Can't you see the Closed for the Day sign?"

"We came in seeing the steam rising from your cauldron. Don't be so stubborn. We're hungry. Let us have a bowl of your sausage soup."

Some tried to talk her into serving them while others turned outright nasty, but she stood her ground. She kicked or pushed out customers coming in or they turned around, offended by her remarks which—hard to tell—might have been curses or proverbs. She opened the lid of the cauldron and blurted out, "This meat is no good. I thought it'd do, so I boiled it but it's no good. That dumb Turk! When did he say he was going to reopen? That old man looks absentminded, but I must give it to him when it comes to his eye for meat. When I ask him where he gets his meat, that cunning fart just wiggles his eyebrows. Go and get the oldsters. Let's have dinner by ourselves today."

The three useless males—me, Uncle Hassan, and Uncle

Amos—blankly watched Aunt Anna setting the table. Because she threatened that she'd kick us out like the other customers if we so much as lifted our fingers.

She was happily playing house. I was her dull child who didn't listen to her, Uncle Hassan was her lazy father-in-law, and Uncle Amos her penniless husband. She was the queen who lorded over us, and offered herself, the family's breadwinner, as the protector of us, the three incapable males. We were supposed to be so useless that we didn't know how to set the table. Our given duty was to sit around waiting for the table to be set and then complain about the food. She said it was okay if I dropped or spilled food as I ate. If I did, she'd gladly put a bib around my neck and spoon-feed me.

"On this good day—I don't know when I'm going to have another good day like this again—what am I doing, waiting on three grown men hand and foot? What a life I have!"

Quietly listening to her complaint was part of our given duties. Uncle Amos predicted that it was difficult the first time, but after closing the restaurant once, she'd do it again.

Aunt Anna lost her temper. "I asked you to play an incapable husband. I didn't ask you to play a nagging mother-in-law. Do you think that I can't wait to starve to death? One day, today, is enough. How can I take a day off again?"

The night deepened. "Closed for the Day" was coming to a close. As if tired, the Closed for the Day sign flapped, almost falling off. Aunt Anna's voice gradually lost vitality. Despite her idleness all day long, her voice was wilted, as if she'd spent the whole day toiling. We couldn't determine whether it was the right thing to go along with her playacting or jump up to clear the table and wash the dishes.

Aunt Anna was at a loss for how to end the day, just like someone who didn't know how to end his life during his final days on earth. Just as we were born without instructions on how to be born, people died well without being taught how. I'd never heard of a person who failed to die. Both Methuselah and the Chinese legendary immortal Dongfang Shuo died eventually.

We journeyed deep into the night, quietly putting up with Aunt Anna's madness that couldn't be more serene. I wished she would make a fuss and cry her heart out as she'd done the night before, as if an earthquake passed through her body. On her body, under a thin layer of clothes, she was supposed to have more scars than I had. But none of us had the courage to see them with our own eyes or talk about them. So Uncle Hassan talked gently to her, like a good father-in-law, as he showed off his eyebrow-wiggling trick, Uncle Amos offered his shoulder like a good husband, and I held onto her thick wrist and put my cheek there, just like a child who didn't know what was going on but was sad because his mother was crying. It would take Renoir to recompose the scene as a happy dinner, but it was closer to Vincent van Gogh's "The Potato Eaters."

Aunt Anna blew her nose loudly on her apron, hooked arms with Uncle Hassan and Uncle Amos, and started giving a lecture on men's proper conduct. That was when the rice shop's second daughter passed by. She turned her head toward us and in the darkness her eyes shone like an animal's. Her eyes had grown sharper.

It had been the same for the children who'd run away from the orphanage but were brought back or voluntarily returned, defeated by the world. When they were plotting an escape, their eyes gleamed with curiosity and expectations. Fresh moisture gathered on their pupils, looking like deep, blue lakes, and lurking in there was the courage to accept both good and evil without discrimination. In short, their eyes were in a state of tension, gentle and taut, just like the eyes of a crouching cat seconds before making a leap. All the runaways, as one, bade farewell before they left, throwing a careful look at where they'd lived until then, as if saying that they might miss it someday but they didn't want to remember it for the time being. They felt fear but it was innocent fear because they didn't yet know how to wield violence to cover up their fear. The beginning of all feelings is pure. Even if the feeling is hatred.

After their return, they bragged about their adventures. It didn't take special insight, however, to realize that they were exaggerating their experience. Curiosity and expectations had turned into disillusion and resignation, and they had to cover them up with futile new hope, so their eyes took on a sharp gleam. I could guess from the eyes of the rice seller's daughter what she'd gone through and what she'd felt. Her sharper eyes were proof that she was returning after confronting a world similar to the one encountered by the runaway orphans. Aunt Anna, who could intuit someone's eyes on her, as if through her pores, turned her head but the girl was gone.

Aunt Anna said, "I wonder if you old guys carry fleas with you. Why is my back itching like I have a heat rash? Wait, who's that fellow out there?"

Someone was rushing by, huffing and puffing. Uncle Amos, thinking this was a good opportunity, slipped out of her hooked arm. Craning his neck to the street, he reported on the identity of the person who'd just passed by. "He's following the tail of a girl and he looks like an ass in rut."

The guy in question was the curly-haired young man. Before long, we found ourselves sitting around the rice shop's second daughter and the curly-haired man. It was because the rice seller Kim, the walking dictionary of swear words, had opened the pages of himself and systematically recited all the entries from the first page on, as he slapped his daughter across the cheek and spat on her. The curly-haired man watched the scene behind a utility pole and after she was thrown out to the street as though she were rice-washed water, he inched toward her and helped her sprawled form up and supported her as they walked down the side road. Uncle Amos, who'd been keeping watch in front of the restaurant all along, beckoned them in. The young man hesitated a little, but spotting me and Uncle Hassan inside, he entered, holding the girl by the arm. She smelled of rice husks.

"Who's this rice weevil of a guy?" Aunt Anna asked nonchalantly as she was taking a seat near the young man. Uncle Amos chuckled. Uncle Amos would sometimes follow Aunt Anna's command to sit in the sun, with newspapers spread out in front of him. He'd pour some rice teeming with weevils on the newspaper and played a watchdog. He was good at killing the tiny, black, firm insects crawling out of the rice heap by crushing them with a fingernail. Uncle Amos had envisioned that the young man, like a weevil, was being crushed with a fingernail.

The curly-haired young man was dark, small, and firm. He removed his hand from the girl's arm and as he placed it on the table, his hand brushed over a porcelain cup, breaking it instantly. As Uncle Amos picked up the shards, he regretted his chuckle.

The rice shop's daughter ferociously rubbed her cheek, where her father's fingerprints were vivid. More ferociously than that, Aunt Anna declared that from then on, she would ban the walking dictionary of swear words from entering her restaurant, and spewed out one proverb after another implying that the one who wielded violence on his own daughter would meet a miserable end. Uncle Hassan brought a towel and patted with it the face of the rice seller's daughter. Her face was puffy, like government-issue rice, inferior to the commercial grade, as she entrusted her face to Uncle Hassan's hand with her upper body slightly leaning on the curly-haired young man. Her eyes had lost their sharpness; now they were duller than Smart-aleck's eyes in ordinary times, and her pale green lips, cracked, looked like a pattern of veins on the blade of a leaf. The young man reached out the tentacles of his gaze and hugged her tightly, just like a big weevil that was hugging a rice grain. The couple looked exhausted. More precisely, they looked hungry.

Aunt Anna let out a sigh. "If you were going to go around hungry, you should've stayed put in your room, just breathing in and breathing out. I knew it! I thought the day was passing without incident. As if it weren't enough to feed three unmannerly men, here I am serving weevils. Closed for the day? Ha! Go take that thing down."

I took off the sign Aunt Anna had pointed to. The couple gobbled up the food prepared by Aunt Anna and let out satisfied burps. They seemed to be in a better mood. The curly-haired man had been throwing glances at Uncle Hassan while he was eating, but there wasn't a trace of an imported pet on him anymore. Any satiated person could be generous and brave. Drinking coffee made by Uncle Hassan, we were pensive, as if we had nothing to say. Nights seemed to exist to teach us that we were part of the universe. The darkness had the talent of swallowing all sorts of white noise. Only then were we ready to hear the sounds we couldn't hear during the day. We paid attention to our internal sounds, realizing anew that they had been there all along. We blamed ourselves for failing to heed them and pledged that we'd never forget them, but when day broke and the sun rose, we completely forgot about our pledge because of the noises that dominated all other sounds.

The handprint was still evident on the girl's cheek. The mark would soon disappear but the handprint imprinted in her soul wouldn't go away as easily. Uncle Hassan commented that a person who loved roses had to put up with their thorns. It wasn't clear whether he said it for the girl or the boy. Either way, we took his words in our own ways. That wasn't enough, so we studied each other's faces.

On the day I left the orphanage, Uncle Hassan said, "We should use others around us as our mirror because we don't have the ability to regard contradictions in ourselves as contradictions. We have no choice but to infer ourselves through others' contradictions. If we don't use others as our mirror, we'll have to live in the realm of the unknown until the day we die." At the time he was referring to the director. I found his words hard to accept.

Other people were other people. Whether they were happy or not didn't concern me. As long as they didn't get involved in my happiness or pain. The director had been involved in my pain only. That was why I wasn't at all sorry about leaving the orphanage.

At this particular moment in the restaurant, though, it began to dawn on me that happiness and pain could be shared, just like air in a room. Six people in the restaurant, including me, didn't seem to be different from each other in nature. It wasn't a feeling that our souls were connected with each other's. This thought alone was horrible. Uncle Amos' soul and mine were linked! I wasn't a murderer, not yet at least. But this was the feeling that seized me at the time: a soul should have an ear to hear the sounds beyond the audible range, I thought, and this idea didn't seem to be far-fetched. I also felt ears did exist in our souls.

Smart-aleck, who was spying on us under the cover of the darkness outside, certainly had an ear in his soul. The problem was that his ear was extraordinarily attuned to only one person: the rice seller's second daughter.

When Uncle Amos dragged Smart-aleck by the ear into the restaurant, the boy was almost in tears.

Uncle Amos said, "You all heard me scream, right? Good God! I thought this rascal was the devil from hell."

We'd all heard him shriek, not long after he left the restaurant for a visit to the toilet. Smart-aleck, seeing him come out, took backward steps, moving from one dark spot to another, all the way into the toilet.

"It was dark, so I thought no one was there. When I turned on the light, this rascal jumped out. I thought a huge mutated maggot was attacking me. Damn it. My soul almost sprang out of my nostrils."

Aunt Anna rubbed Smart-aleck's ear and stroked his hair. Thanks to the exertion of her curative powers, he soon regained his calm. At first, the boy was flustered by the unexpected discovery of his presence, but now he felt humiliated. He looked around the the restaurant as if he'd never been there before. Aunt Anna, befitting the queen of the Chungnam Restaurant, knew what to do.

She put down a rice bowl in front of him and asked no one in particular, "Did anyone invite someone else? I mean do we expect more people?"

We all shook our heads. Finishing our coffee, we watched Smart-aleck, who was chewing his rice as if it were sand. He threw glances at the curly-haired young man. Feeling that the boy's gaze was out of the ordinary, the young man rubbed his firm fists against his thighs. This gesture had no special meaning. His thighs happened to itch, that was all. But Smart-aleck could have taken it as a threat. The yellow-striped cat, having sneaked in without our noticing it, meowed at Smart-aleck's feet. Aunt Anna shrugged and threw a few morsels of meat under the table. I asked Smart-aleck how his project of saving Uncle Baldy was coming along. He shook his head gloomily. A fleeting hatred of the army, society, the state, and things like that floated up in his pupils.

Uncle Hassan sat in a corner and, as he did at home, he dozed with his feet propped up on the table. The two rice weevils ruefully watched Smart-aleck; they seemed to regret that he had taken away their guest-of-honor position. We didn't do anything important, but time kept ticking away. The darkness, growing in the hours called night, became thicker and more solid. The world was quiet and desolate like an unlit lost-and-found center. I'd gradually accepted that the world outside the orphanage wasn't so different from the one inside. In that place where even a tiny sound resonated under the high ceiling, I'd never thought that the world would be like a listless, frightened child like this, although I knew that it wasn't a place to be trifled with. The world I'd imagined was a place that was livelier than this. I'd imagined that even if swindling and conspiracy took place, they'd be swindling and conspiracy worth enduring. But the world didn't amount to much. The swindling and conspiracy that went around in the world were the reenactments of what had taken place among the orphans, only on a larger scale.

In the orphanage, nights couldn't be more insolent. The night wasn't hours that concealed me but hours that erased my being. In the chilly, dark room, in the hours when orphans tried to fall asleep lying on the old, dirty floor, they wished that someone would come and pick them up. They knew very well that they were lost goods, but lost deliberately. But the person who was going to pick them up didn't have to be the one who'd lost them or threw them out. They wished that anyone would pick them up, regard them as something of value, and use them.

The world seemed to be the same. Here, too, people always wanted to be useful. At night, people tried to fall asleep, hoping, with an empty heart, that when the night passed and the morning came the situation would improve, not knowing why they felt the way they did; it was probably a habit evolved over hundreds of thousands of years.

Food was a wonder drug. Smart-aleck looked much more relaxed now. Boldly staring at the curly-haired man, he lifted his finger to point at the young man's face. The two rice weevils exchanged glances.

"Why are your ears like that? They're like Uncle Hassan's."

Uncle Amos, his eyes sparkling with curiosity, examined the young man's ears. Aunt Anna made a fuss, saying that she'd been wondering about just that, too. The girl gingerly touched his ear with her index finger, as if she'd just discovered it. Uncle Hassan was still snoozing. Uncle Hassan's ears were pushed back, as if a roller had gone over them, and stuck flat to his head. Uncle Amos compared the young man's ears with Uncle Hassan's and declared that it was a miracle that two men with those ugly ears happened to be in the same room. The young man said that he'd wrestled years before. The term wrestling floated about in the air. Following the term were its offspring—the drop kick, the headlock, and the Cobra twist. They strangled Uncle Amos's neck and bent all his joints.

"I was a member of my school's sports club. I represented my school for a while, too. It's different from pro-wrestling. Wrestling is a gentlemanly, beautiful sport."

In short, the young man was a magnificent, cruel fellow. The girl seemed to be taken aback, too. Watching her, I wondered how much she knew about him.

All touched the former wrestler's ears and asked questions they had about wrestling. Uncle Hassan was still asleep. I wondered if Uncle Hassan, as a young man, had wrestled, too. Just as Smart-aleck said, the two men's ears were similar. The only difference was that Uncle Hassan's ears hung more naturally. If time passed, the young man's ears might look more natural. Uncle Hassan heard all the sounds in the world with those ears of his. Even with those flat, ugly ears, there was no sound he couldn't hear. There were lots of people who couldn't hear with good ears, but Uncle Hassan, with those ugly ears, could hear sounds below the normal hearing range. By the look of his sleeping face, I gathered, even asleep, he was hearing all the sounds in the world. Uncle Hassan was a person whose soul had an ear, so rare among people I'd come across. Smart-aleck could have that, too. If he'd simply hated his love rival, he couldn't have noticed how peculiar the curly-haired man's ears looked. Smart-aleck might be telling us that both love and hatred were expressions of concern, though different. The girl wasn't embarrassed about her indifference. She, too, found the young man's ears intriguing and put on an expression suggesting that she'd look forward to discovering more about him, like an adventurer who was happy that there still remained an unknown territory to be explored. Aunt Anna seemed thrilled about this new discovery because she spouted one proverb after another that didn't fit the situation, such as "men and melons are hard to know."

A little later, we heard a voice blaming God. The owner of this voice was the proselytizer. He entered the restaurant, sat on an empty chair, and wildly pulled his hair with both hands. Aunt Anna, flabbergasted, gazed down at him but didn't chase him away. It was the first time that we saw him drink. He didn't spoon up any rice from the bowl brought by Aunt Anna, but drank soju with a mouthful of sausage soup in between. He lifted his dazed expression to look around, his eyes revealing that he was eager to spill the beans. Gradually, people had grown closer to each other. With the entry of a new person, the rest divided him up to share equally. The only way for many people to stay together in a limited space was to get closer to each other.

I recalled the family who'd lived in Uncle Baldy's room before they left the neighborhood. They might have been able to live in the tiny room, not because they'd fit themselves together like puzzle pieces as I'd imagined. They could have had the ability to share each other, going beyond the ability to effectively share the space. They could have been absorbed into each other, so six people could have been layered and overlapped to be reborn as a new creature, something like a person who had twelve arms and legs.

The proselytizer was impatient. Before we had the time to ask, he poured out, as if in a confessional, why he was in agony. "I can't remember. No memory!"

The queen of the Chungnam Restaurant and her retinue didn't show any response. We couldn't sympathize with him because it wasn't just one or two things we had a hard time remembering. The proselytizer systematically went over from the time he'd been conceived in his mother's womb to this very moment when he was sitting at the restaurant crying out, "I can't remember. No memory!" He declared that he still couldn't remember. Aunt Anna's face was tragic like an empire's last queen who hopelessly had to look on as her domain fell. A person could despair so serenely if she had to watch an irrevocable event being unfolded before her eyes, I thought.

She lamented, "Why did I take a day off today, of all days? I feel like I'm going through what has been predestined for thousands of years. Will someone explain it to me? Why did these people, even the ones who haven't been here before, come and give me a hard time today, of all days?"

She had a point there but because she had a point her remark was ignored right away. No one in the restaurant was mindful of good points. Uncle Hassan was still asleep. The yellow-striped cat had jumped on a table while no one noticed it, and gazed, with a solemn air, at our pathetic group. The rice seller's daughter frowned at the proselytizer because he'd recently burst into her house and created a scene with her father.

"Tell us," she said, with a touch of irritation. "What is it that you can't remember?"

He grabbed his hair with both hands, and with his elbows touching each other—the most familiar of all human poses of despair—his eyes flashed through the gap of the inverted triangle his arms made. He replied, "I can't remember. No memory! I can't remember the Lord's Prayer."

Aunt Anna imagined what it would be like if she forgot how to make the blood sausage soup, and Uncle Amos, as he crossed himself, wondered what it would be like if he forgot how to make the sign of the cross—later he confessed that there had been times when he was confused about which side to start, left or right, and that God would have forgiven him because it happened during the war—and they believed that they'd be as distraught as the proselytizer. Someone asked, "Why don't you look at the Lord's Prayer in the Bible you have?" He shook his head. He wanted to get back his memory without a crib sheet. He was flustered like a tested person, and tormented himself like someone who was fooled by evil.

Right then, Yujong pressed his face against the glass door to peek in, although it was open. Aunt Anna didn't have the energy to lose her temper, so she went to the kitchen without a word, and the proselytizer was racking his brain to come up with more ways to whip himself. Yujong didn't come in. Only his head crossed the threshold.

"Do . . . do you hap . . . happen to kn . . . know wh . . . where m . . . my mother went?" He stammered more than usual. It was the first time that he wasn't looking for his father, the coal briquette seller. We all shook our heads.

"Mo . . . mother dis . . . disappeared."

Aunt Anna put down new bowls and brought Yujong inside. But he didn't want to eat.

"My sis . . . sister didn't eat, either."

Aunt Anna soothed him. "I'll give you some food to take home. So eat first . . . That's a good boy."

She went out and stood a few steps from the front door. I stood next to her. Closed for the Day. But the restaurant was as busy as ever today.

"I'm so happy. All those people gobbled up the meat that didn't taste any good. Everyone is here, right? The old man Baldy is almost here with us. You can hear him, right? The old man singing the military song with singer Bae Ho's heart-wrenching feeling is already with us with his voice, if not with his body. The drunkard locksmith is fixed right there. Then everyone will be here when that ghostly imam or whatever he's called comes along."

Right at that moment, the imam slipped out of the restaurant. He said that he'd been inside all along. At night, the imam disappeared and his shadow rose and walked around.

"I'm not even surprised," Aunt Anna said, "Will you eat too? No? As you wish. I don't have any rice and soup left, anyway. But I don't know why I feel so empty."

"What? Do you feel empty?" I asked.

She looked down at me and smiled. "If I'd known so many people would show up, I would have cooked better meat. I feel bad about feeding them bad soup. When will we ever get together again like this, like a family, and eat together?"

At that moment, in my heart I put her face in my scrapbook. I put all the faces in the restaurant in my scrapbook. Years later, I would definitely open it and remember this day. If I couldn't have this moment back, I would at least want to recall Aunt Anna's facial expression and the voice I'd seen and heard seconds earlier.

"Now, go to that drunkard old man. Ask him what in heaven's name we're doing."

I approached the old drunkard, who was sitting in front of the grocery as if he were part of the night. I squatted before him and asked, "Who are they?"

"Elephants."

"What kind of elephants?"

"Pink elephants."

"Right. Now I think they look like pink elephants. What are they doing?"

"Passing by."

"They're right there, sitting in the restaurant. What do you mean by 'passing by'?"

He didn't reply.

"Where are they headed?"

He didn't say anything.

It was possible that he knew where they were going but didn't want to tell me, or he himself had no idea where they were headed. My eyes lingered on the silhouette of Aunt Anna standing absently at the door of the restaurant: the ample, soft, sad curving lines created by the puddle of light pouring out of the restaurant. The queen was standing guard to defend her kingdom, the poorest kingdom in the world. Aunt Anna was silently, eloquently saying that just because something was poor didn't mean that it wasn't worth defending. If that was what she really wanted to say, the people in the restaurant would be emissaries who'd rushed from distant lands, from countries equally poor, with the mission of comforting her.

11

There was another butcher shop at the bottom of our neighborhood. When Uncle Hassan closed his shop temporarily, residents had to walk down that far to get meat. The owner of this shop was a man in his forties—it goes without saying that he was Korean—but his business was suspended soon afterward because he violated the law; he sold imported pork as domestic. Now, the residents had to go much farther to buy pork. Their dietary preferences couldn't be changed overnight, so they didn't care for mutton, or they couldn't afford to even look at beef save for birthdays and other festive occasions. They passed by Uncle Hassan's butcher shop with the languid look of carnivores that had been forced to become herbivores.

On any given day, several people peeked into the shop only to turn back, complaining that it was still closed. As they did, Uncle Hassan would look out from his shop. He spent his day there with the doors locked.

Aunt Anna estimated that Uncle Hassan had been in the business for at least thirty years by the way he judged the quality of meat. Some, including Aunt Anna, asked how he could tell imported meat from the domestic. He answered that one could tell by the taste. He meant the meat that didn't taste good was imported and the meat that tasted good was domestic. Aunt Anna's pride was hurt by his pronouncement. "I've touched and worked with enough pork in my lifetime, so much so that I'm sick and tired of it. So why did I ask that grumpy old man in the first place?"

From time to time, a cutting machine salesman showed up at the Chungnam Restaurant. After the butcher shop closed, he'd been trying to convince Aunt Anna to buy an industrial-grade freezer. Before he left our neighborhood, he made a point of knocking at the butcher shop as if it were his duty irrespective of Uncle Hassan's presence there.

Summer deepened and the last of the Three Dog Days was around the corner. Aunt Anna asked Uncle Hassan whether he had any plans for the Last Dog Day. Uncle Hassan, who of course had nothing special planned for the day, silently gazed at her.

"One of my friends is farming in the suburbs and she raises some hogs. Let's go and butcher a hog. It's all right because in-house slaughtering is permitted in her area. How's that sound?"

Uncle Hassan had bought meat from the slaughterhouses at Majang-dong or Doksan-dong. If he slaughtered animals himself, he'd make a bigger profit by cutting out the middle man. He seemed to deliberate her suggestion.

She said, "You should save money as quickly as possible if you want to go on a pilgrimage, the hajj, or whatever it's called."

It wasn't just her coaxing that moved his heart. His meat supplier had announced he'd raise his unit price. All that evening, Uncle Hassan had been holed up somewhere in the house. I searched high and low but couldn't locate him. Before I left the house, I reported to him, wherever he was.

"I don't know where you are but I'm going out. Yujong's mother hasn't come home yet."

I felt as if the walls were nodding. Yujong was sitting blankly in front of Smart-aleck. I felt a sense of déjà vu. The orphanage was a place of simple expressions. There were only expressions that were similar to the ones found on the faces of people whose possessions had been stolen right before their eyes. There were kids with a confident look as though they knew exactly why they had to be in the orphanage. But their true feelings were found on the backs of their heads. The backs of all orphans' heads looked the same.

I went around looking for Yujong's mother with him. Smart-aleck's attention had returned to Uncle Baldy. Like a seasoned detective, I started looking for tips while sticking to the route Yujong's mother would have taken when she left home. Yujong's ability to understand animal speech wasn't of much use now. The animals kept their mouths shut.

The truth of the matter, however, was that I just trailed Yujong. Calmly, he repeatedly went back and forth over the route we'd investigated before. When he arrived at the starting point, he began all over again. Our final point was the bus stop at the bottom of the hill. We didn't go any farther than that. As if it were a cliff at the edge of the world, we didn't take one step beyond the bus stop. If people lifted their feet off the ground and set them on a bus, that was it. The bus stop seemed to be the last place on earth where people loaded themselves onto a rectangular steel box that moved with an internal combustion engine before they disappeared without a trace. We watched many legs disappearing into thin air. When a bus arrived, people disappeared into thin air at knee level. People spewed forth out of thin air, too. Yujong's mother was not among them. Yujong seemed to be a person whose mission was to come and go between the bus stop and his house. He walked silently like a pilgrim. The sun was fair; it was cruel to everyone. Nature never comes across as beautiful to the poor. It is cruel to the poor... because it is so beautiful.

Our neighborhood was already a desert for Yujong. This wasn't a metaphor. He was parched and hot. His body, filled with feverish air, crunched like a well-baked cookie. I was envious of him, though. He had the right to be sad. I, on the other hand, didn't have such a right because I couldn't remember why I'd become who I was. Just as we couldn't be sad about not being born on another planet. I didn't know whom to resent and I couldn't tell for sure whether I had fallen into an unhappy existence from a happy one.

I didn't have a goal or a reason for a pilgrimage. I didn't even know whom to miss. I didn't know what I'd lost, so I didn't have the vaguest idea as to what I was supposed to recover. But I knew one thing. Yujong and I must look similar from the backs of our heads. Yujong seemed convinced. He was walking along the road his mother had taken. He was blaming himself for letting her walk off by herself. This road where no one had stopped her, where no one had held onto her—he was eager to hang onto traces of her. He wasn't coming and going on the same path with the hope that people would volunteer information about when she disappeared. He simply wanted to become his mother.

Uncle Hassan tried hard to send me to school. Uncle Amos snorted. His logic was this: The purpose of education is to instill in students an obsession that they're indebted to society. That is why the educated live all their lives with the thought of doing something good for society, devoting themselves to achieving that goal. He went on to say, "I'd say it's natural to hate school for no reason." I was more envious of the students who were coming home from school in the afternoon than those who were going to school in the morning. I, too, wanted to spend my time somewhere, looking forward to coming home.

I was curious as to why Yujong went to school, so I asked him once. "Why are you getting an education?" He said, "Because, I . . . I'm going to be a no . . . novelist. The no . . . novelist is a privileged person. But he has . . . has to do . . . one thing. The no . . . novelist must testi . . . testify in the court of . . . of the world on behalf of pe . . . people who don . . . don't want to bear wit . . . witness. Just like the doc . . . doctor who suck . . . sucks in bloody pus with his mouth from a pa . . . patient's tu . . . tumor, the nov . . . novelist must wipe off the blo . . . bloody pus flowing in people's so . . . souls. Can you swallow someone's phlegm or sno . . . snot?" I firmly shook my head. "See? No . . . novelists can swa . . . swallow thing . . . things like that." I retorted, "I didn't know they were so gross!"

Yujong walked on a desert all by himself, without a camel or a water pouch. His mother must have done the same. She must have crossed a desert with no one to accompany her. People who went through a desert had ears in their hearts, ears that looked like megaphones, just like a desert fox's. Megaphones to hear with, not to make sounds with. Still, I couldn't hear a thing, not to mention that Yujong couldn't. Special effort was called for to hear what had not been said. Just as Yujong couldn't do anything when animals clamped their mouths shut, we couldn't decipher the adult language yet. Why did she have to leave home? Why did she have to enter a desert? Why did we have to accept all these developments?

Slowly but surely, darkness descended on us. Sitting on Smart-aleck's bench, we greeted the darkness that had descended again. Yujong was afraid of the night. Because when nights repeated themselves, his mother's absence wouldn't be a big deal anymore, because sadder, more intolerable things would occur for sure.

Aunt Anna and Uncle Hassan came out of our house. Aunt Anna declared in a delighted voice, "Boys! I've got something to tell you. I have good news and bad news—which would you like to hear first? Well? Let me tell you the good news first. We'll be going on a picnic. Aren't you happy, just thinking about it?"

None of us looked happy. Uncle Hassan, in particular, looked far from happy.

"Poor things! You don't know how to be happy even when you hear good news! I'll tell you the bad news. We'll have to kill a hog with our own hands. It's a terrible but interesting job. I'm going to invite a lot of people to the picnic. Including the boy who's green with jealousy."

Smart-aleck protested that he wasn't green with jealousy. Aunt Anna ignored him. She addressed me instead, "If you see a fellow who says, 'I'm not jealous of anyone,' make sure to avoid him. He's not human. People are people because they're jealous, they're angry, and they're sad. If you see a person who babbles such nonsense, be suspicious. If he's human but says something like that, he's out there trying to do you in, nine cases out of ten."

Yujong rose to his feet. Aunt Anna told him that he should join our picnic. He didn't reply. Uncle Hassan urged him to eat with us, but he tossed a word in my direction by way of declining, "My sister."

He had a sister. He had someone to look after. His right to remain sad had expired. People's rights are diminished by the fact that sorrow has no expiration date.

On picnic day, an old truck climbed up the side road. The black, grimy exhaust spewing out of its tail spread low above the road. Like a postman who came to deliver some bad news, the truck couldn't hide the look of discomfort. It went past the Chungnam Restaurant and stopped briefly at the real estate agency. The driver, his head poking out of the open window, waved at Aunt Anna.

The truck kept going back and forth as it slowly turned around. The moment it was at a right angle with the road, it slammed into the door of the toilet adjacent to the real estate agency—the toilet was shared by four buildings in the vicinity, including the Chungnam Restaurant. Agent, deathly pale, jumped out of the toilet. Uncle Amos laughed, doubled over. Agent was stabbing the air with a finger while pulling up his pants. The truck, which had retreated a bit, approached him again but he didn't budge from where he stood. The truck honked. Taken by surprise, he fell on his backside. He darted into his office, and with just his arm poking out of it, he kept stabbing the air with a finger. People who'd witnessed the scene asked the truck driver to demolish their dog house or their old lean-to. He expressed dismay, saying that his vehicle was a truck, not a bulldozer. But the truck looked as sturdy as any bulldozer, despite the dented front bumper and peeled-off paint. It looked equal to destroying any structure in the neighborhood.

A huge rubber tub holding kitchen utensils for the picnic was resting in front of the restaurant. Uncle Amos circled it, rubbing his palms, while Aunt Anna filled a Styrofoam cooler with ice and shoved a bundle of food into it. Uncle Hassan brought knives from his shop and Uncle Baldy appeared in a military uniform. Behind him was Smart-aleck, dragging his feet. The yellow-striped cat in Smart-aleck's arms was dozing, indifferent to the picnic.

We loaded the rubber tub and the cooler onto the truck bed, and in the remaining space laid down layers of flattened old cardboard boxes. Uncle Baldy jumped in first, like a platoon commander who'd just conquered an enemy hill, and stretched out his hand toward us. But no one took it to climb in. Each stepped on a wheel or a protruding part of the truck to board. Aunt Anna sat in the passenger seat, cradling the cat in her arms. In the back were five of us: me, Uncle Hassan, Uncle Amos, Uncle Baldy, and Smart-aleck. Yujong hesitated, standing behind the truck. The proselytizer arrived pulling his hair. He assumed that Yujong was hesitant because he couldn't jump onto the truck, so he lifted him up and laid him down where we were. That was how Yujong got onboard. The proselytizer threw a backward glance before joining us last. Uncle Amos shouted, Let's go! I said in my head: Hey, Uncle, we're not headed for Greece.

That was how our picnic began. But all of us squinted under the relentless late-summer sun, and, with no shade to protect us, we helplessly watched our skin being gradually burned. On the slow-moving truck, humidity clung to our skin heavily. Feeling like refugees, not picnic-goers, we looked at the familiar scenes on either side of the side road. The sign announcing Closed for the Day had been put up at the Chungnam Restaurant. The sign waved goodbye to us.

Aunt Anna stuck out her arm from the window and rapped the door with her palm. She tapped rhythmically but it didn't excite us. The truck didn't seem to be equipped with shock absorbers; the ups and downs on the road traveled to us without any mitigation. At this rate, Mongolian spots on our bottoms, disappeared since our babyhood, were bound to come back, I thought. Uncle Amos was delighted as a cowboy, and Uncle Baldy wore a confused smile like a reserve soldier being sent to the front. As the tremors of the engine and wheels reached us, something dormant in us was gradually waking up. We finally felt we were going on a picnic.

At the bus stop, two more people joined us in the rear of the truck: the curly-haired young man and the rice shop's second daughter. They were wearing sunglasses, so we almost passed them by. This time, too, it was Smart-aleck who spotted them. Whenever the truck went over speed bumps, we bounced up and down. Then the imam, sitting in the corner of the truck bed, came into view. So now there were ten passengers in all on the truck bed. In this way, Closed for the Day repeated itself. This happened thanks to Aunt Anna's painstaking preparations. She hadn't been fully satisfied with her day off a while back.

"I told you so," Uncle Amos said, "It's hard for the first time whatever it is, but it's easier from the second time. Wait and see! It won't be long before the Chungnam Restaurant will go bankrupt and close shop. All because its owner loves to take days off."

If Aunt Anna had heard him, she would've poured out a hundred proverbs cursing an enemy and then tossed him out as if she were a shot-put athlete. Just as the driver had instructed, we stayed sprawled on the flatbed, face down, as if we were loads, until we reached the city limits.

The truck was a mass of steel. At the mercy of the truck's radiant heat, we bumped along, with our body parts overlapping as if we were best of friends. An elbow hit someone's chin, a heel was thrust into the pit of someone's stomach, and spittle was smeared on another's head. *Amos, your knee is pressing down on my side. Mr. Proselytizer, will you put on your shoes? It really stinks, you know. Uncle Hassan, your moustache is prickly. Uncle Baldy, can you please put on your hat? My eyes hurt because your head is too shiny. Hey, Boy, don't squirm. You're tickling me, he-he...* Some of our body parts stuck together as if being dried in the sun, like salted fish. Just as the pages of a drenched book stick together in a big lump as it dries, we were stuck together, loaded on the truck as bundles, on our way to what was to be our picnic.

The truck slipped out of the city. The wind carried different smells. The urban smell disappeared and wafts of soil came and went. I asked Yujong to teach me the words describing smells. He gave it a long thought and offered that the words describing taste and smell were interchangeable. Sweet, sour, salty, spicy, and bitter. The transfer of the palate and the olfactory sense. Shared senses. These words rolled off his tongue. If words could be visualized like a cartoon speech balloon, the words coming out of his mouth would be fresh, tart apples, I thought. My face seemed to be shrouded by a soft cloth stained with grass: the smell of soil evoked this sensation in me.

The curly-haired young man and the rice shop's second daughter took off their sunglasses. The marks from their glasses made them look like pandas. They looked around, as if they couldn't believe they'd left the city. The proselytizer gazed at the landscape as if he couldn't care less about the Lord's Prayer at the moment. To tell the truth, I felt like the landscape was gazing at us as much as we were looking at it. We seemed like creatures that were out of place in the landscape. Can I put it this way? I felt like someone who was visiting his hometown after a long absence only to discover that everyone he'd known had either died or moved away.

I'd never imagined my hometown. I could have been born in the countryside or in a city. I could have been born in a poor, dirty house or a well-to-do, clean house. I could have been born in a poor village or an affluent village. Actually, I could have been born in a foreign country, not here. It could have been an unknown country that didn't exist on earth. I loved my indeterminable past—so the past to me wasn't something that was fixed but that could be changed or manipulated as I pleased, although it was more likely that I would let the past remain in an indeterminable state forever—and I loved the memories that couldn't be called out of my brain. I thought it was regrettable that we could live dozens of different lives in our lifetime only when we don't remember our past.

Our feelings on the truck swung between hyperactive and depressed as if we were bipolar patients. Several repetitions of excitement, followed by low spirits, plunged us into exhaustion. Yujong reminded us of the meaning of picnic, *sopung*, *so* meaning strolling and *pung* meaning wind, walking in the wind. Smart-aleck asked what strolling meant. This time around, Uncle Hassan answered: "It means to amble here and there leisurely." Smart-aleck didn't ask what here and there meant or what leisurely meant. Instead of asking, he stood unstably and walked here and there with hunched shoulders. He had nowhere to go. The narrow flatbed was precisely the length and width of our trek and leisure. Smart-aleck laughed merrily. The wind carried his laughter far into the distance. We were in the middle of walking in the wind.

The truck stopped in front of a gigantic zelkova tree. It was so tall that we couldn't touch its lowest branches even when we stood up on the flatbed and stretched our arms high. The tree's muscular trunk, embedded with a hard core, was so vast that it took three or four people with outstretched arms to encircle it, and the tree top was so high that I was dizzy just looking up at it. Under the tree, Uncle Amos, Uncle Hassan, and Uncle Baldy looked no bigger than children.

"This tree is ridiculously old." Aunt Anna sounded unimpressed.

We unloaded our luggage from the truck, upholding our queen's command. The villagers sitting on a pavilion under the zelkova tree welcomed us. There was a well only several steps from the pavilion. The villagers had spread a blue tarp on the well's cement base. They'd put big stones at the four corners of the covering to ensure it wouldn't flap in the wind. They drew up water in a bucket and poured it over the sheet. It appeared that the villagers had done it before because they worked in perfect harmony. An old woman, who was so thin that she might as well have been a whip, embraced Aunt Anna and they wept together for a long time. Our queen must have felt embarrassed about creating a scene; in a low, soft voice, she introduced the old woman as her old friend. An old friend!

A makeshift fireplace was built and a huge cauldron was hung over it. Firewood and kindling were brought, and several buckets and rubber tubs were arranged near the well. The truck driver lay down on the pavilion and fell asleep with his cap covering his face. The village children circled the truck or looked at their reflections in its side mirrors. When they grew tired of all that, they surrounded the sunglasses-wearing couple, gawking at them. The curly-haired man let a child hang from each arm, pretending to be a bodybuilder. The rice shop's daughter giggled with her arms akimbo, like a circus clown. Uncle Baldy gazed at the village and the mountain behind it that looked like a wall screen, and the imam disappeared but he was surely hanging around near us. Uncle Amos sauntered around, as if appreciating the transformation of the nation's bare mountains into lush ones, while Uncle Hassan sharpened his knives near the well. The proselytizer, while standing around with nothing to do, received Aunt Anna's command and followed the whip of an old woman. Yujong, Smart-aleck, and I tailed them. The yellow-striped cat dozed, leaning into the truck driver's side.

A horrible shriek came from the direction of the old woman's house. We couldn't believe that it was a hog's squeal even after we ran and confirmed it with our own eyes. The shriek was the kind that a dinosaur would make, not a mere hog. In the middle of the yard, a hog as massive as Uncle Hassan was thrashing around with its limbs tied up. We pushed a calf-thick pole through its tied limbs and carried the animal on our shoulders as if hoisting a palanquin. The proselytizer had regained his vitality and guided us as if he'd been doing it all his life. He led us in front as if he were a hunter who'd caught a boar. He was much taller than the rest of us, so the hog was hanging at a slant. Yujong and I, supporting the pole at the back, felt an enormous gravity cascading down. Smart-aleck tickled the hog's belly with a stick, and the annoyed animal wriggled and the pole danced up and down. The hog spewed excrement, splattering my face, and Yujong's. This had to be the smell of the sulphurous flames of hell Uncle Amos often talked about.

The proselytizer strode off vigorously like an exorcist who'd just chased away an evil spirit. He paid no attention to the back, so the gravity worked stronger on me and Yujong. Since our pace wasn't even, the hog jerked up and down more erratically, and with the hog pitching and rolling, all of us swayed more irregularly. The new definition of a picnic: zigzagging in the lazy wind, sweating profusely, sharing a space with a thrashing hog.

I felt the well was at the end of the world. When the zelkova tree and the pavilion finally came into view, Smart-aleck tapped the hog on the anus. The animal's curled tail straightened and its entire body turned rigid. Aunt Anna, near the well, waved at us as if welcoming her soldiers coming back with the news of victory. Uncle Baldy started walking toward us. The curly-haired man was still showing off his bodybuilder's skills with a child hanging from each of his shoulders. The rice shop's daughter, surrounded by the girls, let them take turns trying on her sunglasses, while Uncle Amos squatted before wild flowers blooming on a path between rice paddies, swaying his upper body side to side. The imam, who was atop the pavilion gazing at a distant hill, turned his head to look down at us. We could see Uncle Hassan's knives glint in the light.

The moment the reflected light from his knives pierced my

eyes with a transparent chill, the gravity disappeared. Instead, the violent monster was thrashing around on the road. The proselytizer kept walking in front, with the broken pole hanging from his shoulder, and Yujong and I took a few steps backward. Smart-aleck had to run away because the rope tied around the hog's legs snapped. Yujong told everyone that Smart-aleck was the hog's target, so fortunately no one else had to flee. We gathered under the zelkova tree, watching the hog's pursuit.

The animal staggered a minute because it had been tied up for a long time. Smart-aleck threatened it with his stick, but soon realized that this tactic wouldn't work anymore.

The villagers were as happy as a group of theatergoers, saying that no hog had devoured a boy yet. I felt like we were watching a real-life movie, not projected images. The driver, despite the commotion, kept snoozing. The cat squinted and turned her head this way and that to determine where the noise was coming from. If she hadn't heard Smart-aleck's screams, she would have gone right back to sleep. The cat scrambled up, stretched her limbs leisurely, and strolled elegantly to the edge of the pavilion. There, with a dignified mien, she joined the spectators.

Aunt Anna's voice shook with anger, and it was because she couldn't admit that she had such a weakling among her soldiers. "Run, run! If you lose to a hog, you'll have it from me!" Uncle Amos, on the other hand, looked stricken because he was reminded of Zeno's paradoxes. He said, "Ah, fate of that poor hog!"

The scene unfolding before our eyes was a sophism. Who would have imagined that the hog, hung from a pole with its four legs tied up until moments before, would turn into the embodiment of revenge, fiercely pursuing a human being?

Smart-aleck made a wrong turn. As he was dashing through an empty swath of the harvested tobacco field, the hog almost caught up with him. When the two passed through the cornfield, they were out of our sight, hidden behind lush leaves, making us nervous. Looking at the shaking corn, we guessed how far they'd cut through the field. Smart-aleck, escaping the cornfield, switched directions, heading toward the zelkova tree. Afraid that they'd be accidentally drawn into the pursuit, people scrambled up to the pavilion. A breeze passed through the zelkova, scattering down a refreshing rustle.

Smart-aleck was shouting but we couldn't make out his words. Uncle Baldy walked over gently and opened his arms. Smart-aleck jumped into his arms like a soldier who was diving into a trench to dodge artillery shells. Smart-aleck panted in his arms like a prodigal son who had finally come home. It was the curly-haired young man who finally defeated the hog. When he showed off a technique of holding the hog's torso, lifting it high, and then hurling it downward, loud applause broke out. The hog flounced its four limbs as if in a tap-out of a wrestling match. This was a perfect technical fall. We tied up the hog's legs again and moved it to the well. Many expressed opinions on how to kill it. Some said that it should be killed instantly by a hammer, and others asserted that its neck should be slit. They didn't sound very invested, as if discussing whether a wardrobe should be pushed to the right wall or the left.

The proselytizer stepped forward first. He plunged a huge knife into the animal's neck. Then he was at a loss for what to do next. The hog, with the knife stuck in its neck, squealed. Uncle Amos held onto the knife hilt and started sawing off the animal's neck. The neck's diameter was about twenty centimeters. When you multiplied it with Pi, you got about sixty-three centimeters in circumference. Uncle Amos grunted for five minutes and slit six centimeters. At this rate, it would take a hundred minutes to hack off the hog's neck. Uncle Hassan heaved a deep sigh and approached the animal. To let out a sigh, you should inhale as much as you exhale. The imam appeared and blocked him. Uncle Hassan waved him away. The imam shook his head. The imam's shadow loomed over the hog. Did the animal feel serene inside his shadow?

The participants in the picnic, including Aunt Anna, looked

at the hog as if they were bewitched by it. They looked as though they were trying to find in the animal the traces of their lives up to that point. Now the only audience was the hog on the verge of death. It was our witness. One day, the hog would testify in God's courtroom how pathetic the routine of the animals called humans who gladly exhibit cruelty for their daily food.

Uncle Hassan was a true expert. The hog must have suffered less. Some of the meat, hacked off in big chunks, was stuffed in the ice-filled cooler. In a corner, sliced neck and belly meat were roasted, and in another corner a pot of stew bubbled.

Yujong didn't touch the meat, even a morsel. I guessed he didn't eat because of his mother, but my conjecture proved wrong. He said that he'd become a vegetarian. Then he added: When we keep eating meat, we'll eat human flesh some day. I didn't think it was metaphoric. The scars on my body could be the traces of someone's failed attempt to eat me up.

Uncle Hassan washed his knives at the well. He looked unfamiliar to me as he stared at the blades with a languid, sad expression like a soldier who'd just finished a battle at close quarters. A long time ago, he'd been actually in a one-on-one battle. And he couldn't get away from that battle as long as life was a war.

12

When we were leaving the village, Aunt Anna and the whip of an old woman held onto each other and wept again. Saving our final goodbye to the zelkova tree, we exchanged farewells with the villagers.

On the way back from the picnic, I felt as though we'd just cut across the center of an ever-bustling life. From the outset, a leisurely stroll in the wind had been an impossibility.

The flatbed was suddenly filled with acute depressive patients. What made them depressed was Yujong's behavior at the picnic. He'd stuck to his decision to become a vegetarian. Uncle Amos, who couldn't stand the idea, kept pushing meat at him. The proselytizer threw in an upbeat observation, saying that the Lord's Prayer was almost on his lips now that he'd eaten freshly slaughtered pork. Uncle Amos stressed the usefulness of pork to humankind. If he hadn't fibbed that God permitted eating animals, which was recorded in the Bible, Yujong wouldn't have blurted out sharply: "The Bible is the worst invention created by human beings." He went on to elaborate:

So many people have read it for such a long time, but nothing is more useless than the Bible. The Bible didn't prevent wars, murders, and people from oppressing and exploiting others. The world still has innumerable people who are suffering from poverty, starvation, and diseases.

At this assertion, the jaws of Uncle Amos and the proselytizer dropped. The imam and Uncle Hassan seemed worried that Yujong would go on to drag in the Koran, after he was done with the Bible. Aunt Anna stroked Yujong's head, saying that it was impressive that such a small head had thought of a brilliant argument like that. Uncle Amos vented his anger, vowing he'd wait and see what a great novel Yujong would eventually write. Then he said, "Dammit! But why do the words stumbling out of that little Satan's mouth make sense? Oh, God! Please save me."

This was how most of us got depressed. They were depressed because they, like Yujong, believed that the Bible should play certain roles. Because of this cruel belief, the Bible had survived for so long despite its uselessness. But Yujong didn't mock the others' beliefs; he was a small, ugly person who was programmed to be unable to mock others. The only thing programmed for him was that his mother would run away, abandoning him and his sister.

The curly-haired young man and the rice shop's second daughter didn't have their sunglasses on. "I don't care. They're cheap, anyway," said the young man, shrugging like a foreigner. Nothing he had on was of value. The sunglasses were the most valuable thing he had been wearing.

In a corner, Smart-aleck and Uncle Baldy dozed, leaning against each other. The yellow-striped cat slept between them. Aunt Anna didn't poke her arm out of the window. She was asleep in the passenger seat. The truck retraced the route it had taken earlier. The landscape through which the truck passed no longer struck anyone as fascinating. It didn't inspire or excite us.

The truck entered the city. We didn't huddle or crouch on the floor. People looked at us. We didn't budge, as if we were loads on a moving truck. They, too, seemed to regard us as nothing but unusual loads.

We were on our way back home, but I felt uneasy like a refugee who'd just entered an unfamiliar village. Would the village be favorably inclined toward me? Actually, I wouldn't care if it wasn't favorably inclined toward me. I didn't mind as long as it wasn't hostile. When the truck passed the bus stop, Yujong must have felt the same way. He must have thought that the bus stop was also just a stopover point and there was no permanent starting point or permanent final point. What kind of stopover point was the life we were living now? What came before and after our life?

The truck struggled to climb up the steep road. The locksmith, sitting before the grocery, waved at us. He was the only one who welcomed us. The sign reading Closed for the Day was gone from the restaurant. It could have come off of its own accord or someone could have snatched it away. Aunt Anna was sad as if its disappearance amounted to the vanishing of a witness who could testify to our day's journey. She said, "Truth is, we didn't just have fun all day. We brought pork back with us, so it wasn't exactly a day-off for us."

We unloaded our belongings from the truck. The truck repeatedly went back and forth to turn around and didn't disappoint us, ramming the toilet door again. Agent jumped out of it and jabbed his finger in the air; it looked as if we'd been transported to the time before our departure. The driver honked a few times to threaten Agent and also to say goodbye to us before driving down the side road. "Thank you. I had a good time," said Yujong as he turned around to go home. Aunt Anna nodded and held him tight. Yujong trembled in her arms, like a chick. "Don't worry. She'll be back. Yes, she'll come back. No one can wander around for long, leaving an adorable son like you behind," Aunt Anna said, as if she were trying to convince herself. Yujong looked pale and brittle, as though he were a burned-out piece of coal his father sold. He walked away. Everyone stood still until he was out of sight.

I learned by watching Yujong: that the reason we didn't

stammer was not because we didn't have a wound, not because our wounds were healed; it could be because we suffered from a much bigger wound. Yujong didn't stammer after his mother left. He was tortured by the very idea of stammering the word, Mother. Mother. All of us knew that he'd stopped stammering, but none said it aloud. I felt their silence endearing. Yujong must have been grateful for that, too.

If my language was to rip into, crush, and chew up other people like canines and molars, Yujong's language was a wisdom tooth. His language was silent, mumbled, trapped in the gums. The wisdom tooth, lying sideways or upright, would be trapped in the gums, aging immaturely and then rotting. Yujong would feel the pain forever.

Uncle Hassan took his portion of the meat and went to his shop. The imam had disappeared and the proselytizer returned to his hair-pulling. The curly-haired young man and the rice shop's second daughter were anxious because they didn't know where to go, while Uncle Baldy and Smart-aleck went to their respective homes. Aunt Anna set out to boil the meat, using me and Uncle Amos as her servants. "If you're going to stand around like that, doing nothing, come here and help me," she addressed the curly-haired man and the rice shop's second daughter, conscripting them into service as well

That night, I asked Uncle Hassan, who'd finished his prayer: "Do you meet God every day? Why doesn't He come to me?"

He was silent for a moment before he offered, "God is dormant in you. No need to wake Him up by force. Let Him wake up, blinded by light."

"How can I make Him wake up, blinded by light?"

"Polish your soul. Make it shine as you'd polish the wooden floor, as you'd polish a mirror until it accepts a tiny glimmer of light and flashes it back like the sunlight."

As for me, I wouldn't have minded if I didn't wake up, sleeping forever. While you are asleep, you have a hope that you'll wake up.

The butcher shop opened for business. Uncle Hassan did what he had to do, as he'd done in the past. He changed into work clothes, wiped down the scale and the butcher block, and sharpened the knives. He cut up fat-trimmed chunks of meat, wrapped them in newspapers, and handed them over to his customers. When he returned home after a day's work, he snoozed in his familiar posture, perched on a chair with his feet propped on the table. When he woke up, he walked like a ghost to his room and fell into a deep sleep.

I still took all my clothes off to reflect every corner of my body in a small mirror, or sat in a small chair on the veranda, which commanded a good view, off the kitchen door, and gazed out at the murky sky, the poor neighborhood, and the gray city, just as Uncle Hassan did from time to time. When I felt as if I'd been sitting there for thousands of years, I thought that life was infinitely repeating itself, instead of going forward.

A gloomy shadow of clouds was cast over another poor neighborhood on a distant hill across from ours. Fate there was the same as fate here. People were moving away from the hill on the other side, but to me it looked as if it were turning into a desert.

There was a desert inside a person, too. Some parts of my body, to which I failed to pay attention, had already turned into a desert, and mostly it was the part called the heart, invisible and untouchable. If the sand dune was a topography created by the wind, the scars in my body were a topography created by my years on earth. I was still young, and for this reason I didn't want to live for a long time. I didn't know what death was like, and in the same vein I didn't know what life was like, but I didn't especially care to know and felt I wouldn't mind much if my life ended right then and there.

Aunt Anna said that a human life span was too long. After people learned the word Mom, acquired hunting skills, and gained the ability to reproduce, they wasted their entire lifetime learning and doing bad things. Aunt Anna said that it'd be the same if the average life span was twenty years. According to her, people would try to reproduce from the age of four and commit misdeeds from the age of five. Just thinking about it made me shudder. A four-year-old playboy! A five-year-old highway robber! The life span had nothing to do with the soul. What was important to us wasn't how long we stayed on earth, but what and how we loved while staying here. But I had never experienced love.

I grew thirsty as I studied the faces in my scrapbooks. They looked similar, but I felt that I still had many faces to collect. Maybe I was looking forward to meeting a face that contained all the expressions to be worn by human beings.

Smart-aleck was glum. It had begun to dawn on him that he would never find a way to rescue Uncle Baldy. He started saying again, "Who cares? I'm going to die."

I wanted to tell him that now I understood why he was spitting out those particular words as if by rote. He gently stroked the back of the yellow-striped cat. The cat's tail shot up. The cat, with narrowed eyes, purred. This green-eyed cat would see the world dyed in green. To the cat, Smart-aleck and I should look like green monsters.

Uncle Baldy came to visit Smart-aleck on his bench. No matter how hard the old man tried to coax him to take a stroll with him, the boy didn't budge. He looked like he couldn't be bothered with anything in the world. It was a common expression worn by Smart-aleck, but this time in particular, he looked rather tragic. A tragic laziness!

So Uncle Baldy ventured out to take a walk by himself. Smart-aleck craned his neck to confirm that he had disappeared around the bend of the side road.

"Let's go. I have something to do," he said.

We went to Uncle Baldy's room. The door yielded easily. When I hesitated at the doorway, Smart-aleck scowled. The yellow-striped cat kept watch for us. I entered the room for the second time in my life. It was the room where six family members had lived, surely absorbed into each other to become a single body. As though he'd been planning to do just this for a long time, Smart-aleck entered the room with purpose and searched the room systematically. He lifted up the floor mats, patted down the gaping wallpaper, and pulled out all the drawers of a small wardrobe. Wherever his hands touched, the songs that had been absorbed there floated out. All the objects in the room looked rigid, like soldiers preparing for battle, probably because Uncle Baldy's songs had seeped in.

As he circled the room, Smart-aleck grew calmer. He took out Uncle Baldy's military uniform, military boots, and khaki underwear and socks. And the khaki belt, the silver buckle, the peaked field cap, and the worn-out epaulet. We gathered them up and left his place. We briefly sat in silent tribute near the bench before burning up all of Uncle Baldy's belongings, using newspapers as kindling. The objects looked like items left behind by a dead person, and we felt like priests performing a rite. An era was flaring up. A person's past went up in flames, billowing out dark, noxious smoke.

The smoke soon died down and large, red flames flickered, like a tongue stuck out by the earth. Smart-aleck looked down at the city. His eyes, stinging with the smoke, were red. An orange celestial evening streak disappeared in his eyes. A person's life was valuable, so much so that it could be exchanged with Mother Nature. Smart-aleck said that he'd like to burn up everything that would remind Uncle Baldy of the military and the war.

He said, "If Uncle Baldy could recover his memory after I do this, I don't care if he doesn't get what little compensation he deserves. He didn't go to war hoping for compensations, anyway. There're people who've been robbed but there's no one who robbed them. That's the way of the world. I came to understand that much. But we shouldn't let our memory be stolen from us because it is the privilege given to every one of us."

Uncle Amos came over and shed tears. He glossed it over, saying that it was because he'd eaten ginger. Uncle Amos had almost lost his ability to lie. Soon after I arrived in the neighborhood, I'd asked Uncle Hassan about Uncle Amos, and he answered, "Don't avoid a person just because he's timid, clumsy, and narrow-minded. He'll criticize you, deceive you, and make fun of you, but he'll be the only one to sympathize with your pain and sorrow from the bottom of his heart."

I believed his words.

That night Uncle Baldy didn't sing. From then on, he ignored Smart-aleck. It was possible that he'd really forgotten him. Smart-aleck seemed to have traded his shared memory with him for Uncle Baldy's past. Ramadan began. Uncle Hassan fasted, not eating anything while the sun was up. He had a bite at night and at dawn. Uncle Hassan was getting on in years. It was the month of fasting that he'd observed all his life, but his body, despite his faith, didn't adjust to fasting very well. I saw him dry heaving several times. A few times, he actually threw up all he'd eaten. He spoke incoherently:

"I should send you to school . . . Bombs exploded right next to me . . . In Istanbul, there's a notorious old prison called Yedikule . . . At one point, my dream was wearing a gentleman's hat . . . Here we are, at Seoul's gecekondu, a slum where godforsaken poor people are concentrated . . . If your tribe's ancestor was a bear, our ancestor was a female wolf. I grew up looking at the portraits of Ataturk and Fevzi Çarkmak . . ."

When I told Aunt Anna about it, she wiped down my cheeks with her palms. She said, "Don't worry. He's old and he's not feeling well. That's all. I babble nonsense, too, when I'm drained of all energy. That damn old Turk! He should know his own condition. Fasting, ha!"

The landlord of the butcher shop and Agent came over to see Uncle Hassan, who was cutting up some pork. I was looking at my scrapbook in front of the butcher shop. The landlord told Uncle

Hassan that he was going to raise the deposit and the monthly rent.

Uncle Hassan, putting down the knife, asked politely, "I've never been late on rent. What's this all about?"

"As I said, I want a higher rent. I haven't raised it for the past two years, so it's not as if I'm being unreasonable, you know."

Agent nodded vigorously to indicate that his companion was absolutely right. Agent addressed the landlord, "Nowhere else can anyone find a place with such a low rent. You should have raised it a long time ago, but you're so soft-hearted."

Uncle Hassan ignored Agent. He politely asked the landlord, "How much do you intend to raise it?" As the landlord hesitated, Agent raised his right index finger. He meant 10 million won. They were not so much demanding a higher rent as demanding that Uncle Hassan vacate the place. Uncle Hassan finally caught on. Realizing that a negotiation would be useless, he silently saw them off. Uncle Hassan was given two months' notice. His butcher shop was destined to disappear in two months.

That evening, in the middle of eating Turkish meatballs, Uncle Hassan put down his fork and sat immobile. He seemed to feel like retching. The flesh around his mouth twitched.

He said, "It happened during the war. Our supply was cut off and our company was isolated. The enemy was strong and we were exhausted. I couldn't even feel hunger. With my stomach completely empty, I felt like I was a walking ghost. The mountain was treeless and there was nowhere we could hide from the shelling. All we could hope for was that the shells would miss us on God's blessing. A shell exploded right next to me. I was flung into the air and then hurled down. When the smoke cleared and there was a lull in the enemy's shooting, I realized that something was in my mouth. I cautiously chewed it. It was sweet. Only later did I realize that I'd eaten torn human flesh from the bombing. It began to dawn on me that war made humans eat humans. It forced human flesh into your mouth. Today, this meat tastes exactly like the human flesh I swallowed then."

Later, I relayed this story to Aunt Anna, and she said that she'd expected as much. "I knew it! That old Turk has a face advertising he can kill and eat people. I told you, didn't I? He's going to raise you and eat you up. So be careful."

I could see Agent trotting to and fro outside the restaurant. Aunt Anna gave him the evil eye. "When there's a rumor of redevelopment, even this neighborhood is agog with excitement. If they tear down old houses and build new ones, they'll get bigger compensations, I hear. The building owners have nothing to lose. Money can be borrowed in one way or another for that. You should know this. Where we live is not the Republic of Korea. This is just capitalism. This guy capitalism has no manners. You shouldn't rely on capitalism, you see? You're going to get hurt in the end."

Uncle Hassan grew weaker by the day. He didn't skip prayers or stop fasting. I tried to coordinate my mealtime with his. He didn't want me to do that, and I had to eat all alone. In these moments, I felt that people were born to be solitary. When Uncle Hassan sensed that I was looking at him blankly, he said, 'I'll get back on my feet when Ramadan is over."

When the fast was over, he was supposed to shut down his shop. For the first time, I began to worry about my future. I wouldn't have if I'd been alone. It was a future to share with someone, not a future for just myself.

"Oh, dammit! It's not long since he started supporting you, and here you are worrying about how to take care of him!" This was how Uncle Amos put it.

I wouldn't deny that I had worries in my heart. But these were worries I was willing to embrace. Sitting on the veranda off the back door, I watched the neighborhood on the hill across the way being demolished. The muezzin's voice ululating from the mosque would travel that far. But the mosque and the rest of the world would remain safe and sound forever. Only people would fall. I'd watched, from the beginning, how the neighborhood on the opposite side, a twin of my neighborhood, was being torn down. Someone built a steel tower over there. Its purpose seemed to appeal to the heavens that the demolition be stopped. The steel tower was soon taken down as well, as if a hair clipper razed the back of someone's head. A variety of machinery destroyed the old, dirty houses to smithereens. It was amazing to see a neighborhood being erased, starting from the bottom of the hill. I found it amazing to see how a neighborhood was turning into ruins. People living over there couldn't see the spectacle. They had to leave without a backward glance. Or maybe their houses would have gone down in their hearts, so they wouldn't have had to confirm it with their own eyes.

My scars throbbed in response to the hilly neighborhood that was being torn down.

Touching my scars, I asked them, "Is this how you guys feel?" They didn't answer. I went around carrying a scrapbook but I didn't know what kind of face I was looking for.

Uncle Hassan's face had turned ashen. Whenever he prayed, I was afraid that he'd never get up again, prostrated like that. When he elegantly lifted his hands, palms up, and closed his eyes, peace descended on his hands.

Opening my scrapbook, I asked Yujong's father, the coal briquette seller. "Can you tell who's Japanese?"

He wiped his blackened face with his blackened hand. This was a habit he had when he stopped to catch his breath while pulling a handcart piled high with coal briquettes. He picked a face with the tip of his finger. I asked, "Why did you select him?" He answered, "He looks like a typical Jap." I asked him what he meant by that, and he answered, "He looks sly, if you know what I mean." I pointed at a face that looked sly and asked why he thought this person wasn't Japanese. He cocked his head. His wife hadn't returned yet. I told him that the person he'd picked was Korean. "Darn it! Jap or Kook, we're the same. But his situation must have been as hopeless as mine. Poverty was written all over his face."

Rain fell and the temperature changed overnight. After struggling to fight off the suffocating heat of the dragging summer days I was so tired that I didn't feel like lifting a finger. Uncle Hassan's gait grew unsteady. He walked like someone who was wading across a swamp.

I opened my scrapbook and asked the rice seller Kim, the walking dictionary of swear words: "Can you pick out who's an Iraqi?"

He snorted. He pointed at a face right away. The face he chose had reddish skin, thick eyebrows, and a moustache. His deep-set eyes looked hollow, accentuated by double eyelids.

"I'm sorry, but he's Korean."

The dictionary of swear words didn't believe me. "In heaven's name! Can't believe there's a bastard like this among Korean seeds. Dog . . ."

Before his mouth could call up all the swear words in the world involving dogs, I interrupted him. "He's forty-two years old. He lives in Hoengseong, Gangwon Province. Occupation, farmer. He grew a moustache because he adored Vivian Leigh in *Gone With the Wind*. The guy who seduces her in the movie is a dandy with a moustache."

He asked who Vivian Leigh was. I told him that all the men in the world were dying to kiss her. "Plague on him! This guy, that guy, every guy is a sucker when it comes to women. From the beginning, I thought he looked like a farmer."

Uncle Hassan grunted all night long, although Uncle Baldy didn't sing. I surreptitiously touched his forehead. He didn't have a high fever.

I opened my scrapbook and quizzed Agent about the nationality of a face I was pointing to. That face had dark skin, prominent cheekbones, a round and upturned short nose, and thick lips. Agent let slip a smile and said, "Isn't he African?" He said that he couldn't say which country the guy was from because there were so many newly independent countries over there. He listed African countries he knew—Kenya, Ghana, Nigeria, the Republic of South Africa, Ethiopia—and said that he was sure the guy was from one of them. But the person in question was Korean. "If this guy is Korean, I bet he's a mongrel," he said. I proved that the owner of that particular face was a pure-blood Korean. "You see his face here in this picture? He's with his parents and siblings. They are all alike, aren't they?" Agent shrugged and said, "Our country is tiny but look how many weird-looking people we have out there!" He added, "That guy, he must be from a well-to-do family. See how smooth his skin looks!"

I rearranged the faces in my scrapbooks. I put presumably typical Korean faces in the center of a page, as a sort of standard, and placed look-alike faces in all directions, creating a picture. This was something like montage art. But I wasn't looking for an accidental effect; it was an effort that had a clear goal. I was meaning to make a world atlas with these faces, arranging them so that they looked similar to the ones next to them. A small difference was all that was required; a nose a little higher or lower, eyes a little deeper or shallower, cheekbones a little more prominent or flat, skin lighter or darker.

As time passed, the faces I put in the scrapbook couldn't look more different from the first standard Korean faces. This was similar to a joke that a ten-year old had a friend who was fifteen, who had a twenty-year-old friend, who had a thirty-year-old friend, and so on until the ten-year old was a friend with a hundred-year old. If there was a difference, my effort wasn't as insolent as the joke.

In my map of faces, a Korean became a Chinese or an Arab. Another Korean would cross continents to become an African or a European. Some could have lived in a log cabin in Scandinavia, built an igloo in the North Pole, or run a ranch in Patagonia. Others could have slept in a hammock under the shadow of a Banyan tree or in a straw-floor hut in the jungle. Still others could have seen the Southern Cross or the North Star, could have strolled on a desert or on the sea, and could have moved around on the back of a camel or a yak.

I decided to show the completed map to Uncle Hassan. He had left home as usual but couldn't open his shop. He gazed at his workplace for a long time before coming home. He wandered around our apartment nervously, like someone who was looking for a place to hide, and fell asleep, exhausted like someone who'd just finished strenuous physical labor. The sunlight streaming in from the window caressed his face, and his chest rose up and down irregularly. Since it was still the fasting period, he didn't take a sip of water. His parched lips had begun to crack and his moustache lost luster. I'd put my finished map near his head, waiting for him to wake up in time for his prayer. When he woke up to pray, he absently gazed at my map.

"It looks like you've found invisible dots connecting people."

"You're the one who taught me that. Look, Uncle. Look at your face. You look more Korean than any Korean and look more Turkish than any Turk."

"You mean that it's hard to tell whether I'm Korean or Turkish."

"You're right. It's become difficult to tell where you're from. Not everyone can be like you."

"In your picture, everyone can become like me."

"That's why it's a picture. In reality, it's an impossible dream."

"You put the reality you know in your map."

"Just because you know something doesn't mean it exists. Love, friendship, peace, freedom . . . We know the words but we've never seen them in real life."

"I've never taught you that. But I guessed that you'd realize something like this."

"So you knew I'd become like this . . . To become the self-hating, despicable person that I am."

Uncle Hassan sighed. "No one made you hate yourself. It's you."

He pulled me down and buried me in his broad chest. His chest wasn't firm.

"Your scars aren't simply scars. They are where history is imprinted. All my scars are also imprints of my personal history."

I waited for him to go on, but that was all he said. The scars are where history is imprinted. This remark incited an odd feeling in me.

After his prayer, Uncle Hassan fell asleep again. I lay next to him. There was nothing I could do. As I lay there, my bones rattled. I knew that the skeleton lying in my body was hurting. I wanted to gather up the bones in my body, arrange them perfectly in their original skeletal shape, and love them. Uncle Hassan's skeleton was rattling as well. It was about to break out of him, having waited so long for him to take it out. That would happen, of course, only after the skeleton had lost him, the object of its love.

I took my picture to the Chungnam Restaurant. Aunt Anna was an art lover who happily accepted any new art. "I'll put it up on this wall. It'll cast a curse on my customers who deserve it." I didn't mind that my artwork had turned into her talisman. It was because Yujong said: You should know how to use words, and if you don't, they might become an incantation. Language, depending on how it is used, can become words or an incantation.

I put up the world atlas made of faces under the menu board on the wall, as directed by Aunt Anna. Is it possible to tell to which tribe, to which nation, a person belongs with his face alone? The conclusion is no. Therefore we don't have the inborn ability to categorize people into races. This means that we only have the ability to regard humans as solely humans. It means that classifying people into black, white, and yellow is a result of training after birth. We also acquire the ability, after birth, to tell whether someone is rich or poor: the ability to tell a poverty-stricken face from a face exuding affluence. If this human ability comes from God, how great and intelligent He is! He doesn't give humans, before birth, the abilities that may come back to Him as criticism.

I asked the old drunkard. "Who am I?"

"Elephant."

"What kind of elephant?"

"Pink elephant."

"What am I doing?"

"Passing by."

"Where am I headed?"

He didn't say anything.

I pulled down the neck of my T-shirt to reveal the scar below my collarbone. This scar was where history was imprinted. I pointed at my exposed scar and asked, "Do you have a key that fits this lock here? A magic key you can insert into it and twist to make it disappear without a trace. Do you have a key like that?"

13

That autumn, Uncle Hassan lost the strength to go on. Just as a pent-up sob bursts out, the power of intervening years flushed out of his body. The houses high on the opposite hill had come down, and it was impossible to picture the place before the demolition. Uncle Hassan went to work early, as if by habit, but returned right away. He didn't unlock the door of his shop. Standing in front of it, he looked bewildered, like a foreigner at an unfamiliar tourist site. He peeked in as if he were looking at someone else's workplace and studied the appliances as if he were looking at someone else's belongings. Soon his butcher shop building would be razed to the ground. No more meat would be placed under the knife with its hilt stained with his sweat, and no more meat would be slapped on the butcher block. It was possible that he was glimpsing himself, a phantom, engrossed in work inside. And he might be gradually admitting to himself that his work was completely a thing of the past. I'd say he went to his shop not with a desperate heart but with the intention of coming to terms with his situation.

Uncle Hassan came and went like a ghost. I was afraid that his shadow would disappear as he walked around. I knew why he came and went like that, but I didn't show that I was aware of it. Scars can be hidden under clothes, but if you don't have a limb, the truth is bound to come out however hard you try to conceal it. A human body is mysterious, because even a missing part is revealed. Uncle Hassan acted like a person who had a missing part. He hoped that I'd overlook why he was dragging his tired self around and what drove him to do so, although it was obvious for anyone who was paying half attention.

Uncle Amos asked me, "Where on earth is Hassan wandering around?"

"Uncle Hassan is looking for someone who'll replace him. For me. So I wouldn't be sent back to the orphanage."

I learned this way of speaking from Uncle Baldy. He'd stop by at the bench in front of Smart-aleck's house when the boy wasn't around. He sat and lay down exactly where Smart-aleck normally sat and lay. He asked me how the boy was doing but made sure that I wouldn't mention his visit to him.

"It's not that I have other reasons. I know why he did what he did. I don't have the nerve to disappoint him. I haven't recovered my memory yet. At least, I don't want him to think he failed."

On the day when a big prayer meeting was held at the mosque, Uncle Hassan left home, his face deathly pale, and returned with a middle-aged man before dinner time. The visitor had sharp eyes and a moustache. He nodded at me—that was all. The two talked and when prayer time came, they prostrated on the floor together, side by side. Afterward, they went to the Chungnam Restaurant with me. The visitor didn't show any reluctance about going into a restaurant selling pork dishes.

Uncle Amos muttered, "In this country, all the Muslims devour pork as if it's nothing." Aunt Anna sat next to me and squeezed my hand. Uncle Hassan revealed his plan for how to dispose of the appliances at his butcher shop. Uncle Amos suggested that he rent another space and run a butcher shop as he used to. Uncle Hassan said that he no longer had the confidence to handle the meat.

Uncle Amos and Uncle Hassan seemed to share a certain understanding without speaking. They'd had nothing to take and nothing to leave behind if they were to die right then and there. I felt as though I was being excluded from them. While Uncle Hassan talked, he didn't throw me a glance, not once. As if in agreement, they acted as if I weren't there, but then it wasn't as if they brought up anything that concerned me. They were carefully making a detour, like passersby who encounter an abandoned child in the street. It seemed that I didn't have a say in the matter of my own fate. It seemed as if no fate had been given to me from the outset. The thought that it was because I was an orphan, not because I was a minor, bothered me.

Their voices echoed in my ears. Consonants and vowels arrived separately, no meaning reaching me. Surrounded by the noise, I looked outside, where darkness was gradually descending. I couldn't claim that I'd had no idea that things would come to this. I was a person fated to be the way I was. The visitor advised Uncle Hassan that he leave for a pilgrimage on what he'd make by liquidating his appliances—the hajj—the term they used referring to pilgrimage. Uncle Hassan neither agreed nor disagreed.

Uncle Amos wildly gestured in excitement and spilled his cooled coffee on me. Aunt Anna peeled off my shirt. I hunched my shoulders. The visitor, with a surprised expression, looked me up and down. To be more precise, he gazed at my scar-strewn body. He frowned and narrowed his eyes. He seemed to study every scar I had. Aunt Anna wiped me with a towel.

"How terrible!" the visitor said as he pointed at the scar below my collarbone, "Child, do you know how you got that?"

I shook my head.

"This somehow looks familiar," he said, and turned his head to look at Uncle Hassan.

Uncle Hassan didn't say a word. I imagined that the visitor had a scar like that. He stayed late into the night. As he left, he waved goodbye to me in the dark.

But before he strode off, he said, "Now I remember. About your scar. I was wondering why it looked so familiar. Hassan has a scar just like that."

Uncle Hassan lay immobile in the room. He didn't have a fever but had a dry cough. He seemed to have a headache by the way he pressed his temples with his thumbs. His parched face, with dark spots here and there, looked like a mask. What made him stay in this foreign country for decades? Why couldn't he leave? Why hadn't he returned to his homeland? Why was he getting old all alone and enduring his illness by himself, so lonesome? I wanted to see Uncle Hassan's scar. The scar that was said to be similar to mine. The similarity between the scars didn't mean that our fates were similar, but I thought I could find from his scar something I hadn't known.

I whispered into the ear of sleeping Uncle Hassan, "Please don't abandon me. I hope you're my last orphanage." But even Uncle Hassan had a fate he couldn't do anything about. I didn't resent him, because I could understand him. What I should criticize was not him, but fate that had descended on him.

Uncle Hassan, like the imam, was fading away. I thought this was how a farewell worked. He was still fasting. Ramadan wasn't over yet. Befitting the tribe that had lived in vast plains and deserts, his people were accustomed to self-abuse and self-denial. The orphanage had been busy during the holidays and at the end of the year. On holidays, volunteers materialized out of the blue to clean, cook, and teach us all sorts of games. Some taught us how to set food on the ancestral-rite table and how to bow in front of it. At the end of the year, we were always gathered in the frosty front yard, had our photos taken standing behind ramen boxes and gunnysacks of flour, and were lectured about how the world was a place worth living in. Some children acted up, hoping to draw attention, and most of what they could come up with was hurting themselves. They deliberately tripped on the stairs and tumbled down, or they picked a fight with other kids to get hurt.

Then, the visitors said, in unison, that we should know how to love ourselves. They said that if we didn't love ourselves, we couldn't break away from the thought that life wasn't worth living. They were cowardly. Loving oneself was the final stronghold. This advice had to be given to people who were exhausted with loving the world and loving other people. This advice was good for people who were tired of loving and had nothing more left to love. This advice would be comforting for people like that. I wanted to tell Uncle Hassan that he could love himself, that he had every right to do so, that people who didn't have the right talked about love for so long, and that people who didn't have the right had distorted self-love for so long.

Uncle Hassan was the first person who hadn't been suspicious of me. He knew what I was thinking. This happened one day when we were taking a walk through the park. My heart ached because of some instinct. The brilliant sky, the green trees, and the life pregnant in them. Isn't there a moment when the world becomes a clear meaning and bursts upon us like a shower of rain? With the moment over, the moment when even my soul seemed soaked in a fleeting rain, my eyes welled up with tears at the thought that I was just passing through this precious, beautiful world. Uncle Hassan understood why I was crying for no apparent reason. He said that we should be able to shed tears at the sight of beautiful things. He added that to do so, we should be able to perceive that the world was a beautiful place.

The proselytizer came to see Uncle Hassan, saying that he'd heard about his illness. The proselytizer looked haggard. He said that there were some holdouts in the neighborhood where the demolition was going on. He explained that he led prayer meetings for the holdouts together with a pastor from a pioneering church. I asked him whether he could remember the Lord's Prayer, and he answered, reddening, "I think you'll understand me some day. I don't mind it at all now. It's okay if I don't remember it. That's just one of many prayers. I've so much to pray for and there are so many prayers for which I'm waiting anwers." He promised that he'd pray for Uncle Hassan's full recovery.

The curly-haired young man and the rice shop's second daughter came to visit as well. The young man said that he was working as an assistant to a night club stunt man who pulled heavy stuff with his teeth, among other gigs. He looked bashful as he revealed that he might be able to get married soon, now that he had a regular income. I touched his ear that looked the same as Uncle Hassan's and it wasn't as rigid as I'd expected. Firm softness. That might have been the secret that attracted the girl.

Uncle Amos said that he'd released the bird that had been imprisoned in the room. "I was scared. My hand shook. But my heart soared when the bird flew, barely flapping its wings, like a young bird that has just learned to fly, but it finally flew away determinedly." I decided to swallow his lie again. He looked relieved like a soldier who'd safely carried out his final mission. Uncle Amos had to be one of those who weren't used to loving themselves. What was left to him was probably to reflect on his mistakes that he could ignore while carrying out his lifelong mission of lying.

I looked up at the sky with Uncle Amos. In that sky, probably such birds—be they the legendary Phoenix, Roc, or Janka—could have flown for a long time, scissoring through the empty air. There was no path in the empty air because the air itself was a path. There was no path on the ground because the ground itself was a path. We watched, in admiration, the empty air being shattered in glittery specks and cascading down like a shower of falling flower petals. "This is as beautiful as the Greek sky." Ah, Uncle Amos! What he'd released wasn't a bird but the young man Amos who was crisscrossing the sky on an outdated plane.

On the last day of Ramadan, Uncle Hassan collapsed at the Chungnam Restaurant. That was the day when the butcher shop had officially become a place that had nothing to do with him. The contract had expired and the remaining appliances were handed over to a used goods dealer. Nothing there belonged to him anymore. Even memories didn't seem to be his. He threw up blood. He spat out phlegm speckled with berry-red blood. When I entered the restaurant, Aunt Anna, sitting blankly with reddened eyes, jumped up. She told me that an ambulance had been called and Uncle Amos accompanied Uncle Hassan to the hospital. I looked into Aunt Anna's bloodshot eyes. She was flustered. But she didn't see in my face an expression she'd expected.

"Oh my goodness! Who's done this to you? . . . Now come over here. The old Turk was sitting right here, on this chair. He collapsed as he tried to stand up. Now, touch this chair. Cheap sponge is under this dirty fake leather. That's why the chair remembers the person who was sitting here. Look! When someone presses his butt here and then gets up, he leaves a mark. Isn't it amazing that this looks like a heart? God hides life's secrets like this in a place we're most embarrassed about, a place that's part of ourselves but we can't see with our own eyes, like our bottoms that could be seen only by other people."

I touched the chair where countless people had put down their butts. As Aunt Anna observed, the chair where Uncle Hassan had sat until moments before had an imprint of a heart.

Leaving the restaurant, I looked around, confused about where to go next. I walked down the alley, the same alley I'd walked along the first day when I trailed Uncle Hassan to this neighborhood. Life might be nothing but numerous reenactments of life's archetypes. At the bus stop, I got on a bus without knowing where it was headed. I wandered around the city, standing in the empty air off the ground, at the height of a person's waist.

Outside the windows, the cityscape passed by. I got off at a random stop and transferred to the subway. Then I came out onto the street once again and took another bus. I carefully looked at the old seats on the buses and the subway. There, too, were secret patterns. The same thing happened to rigid seats. The seats, in faded colors with paint peeling off, bore some marks. Any place where people's bottoms had stayed contained secret patterns, though faintly. God left his traces in trifling things. But I couldn't erase the feeling that I was separated from the world, although I still belonged to it.

At the bus terminal, I drank a soft drink the bus driver handed me. I gave him the name of the hospital Aunt Anna had mentioned to me. He directed me in detail how to get there. I got on another bus departing from the terminal. Looking at the passengers' behinds, I thought: Don't those bottoms hold the single expression that contains all human expressions that I've been so eager to find?

Uncle Hassan was lying in a cot in the emergency ward because a room wasn't available for him yet. Uncle Amos, all alone, was watching over the unconscious patient. He stroked my head.

During his hospitalization, Uncle Hassan's condition deteriorated. They said he had pneumonia. Ramadan was over but Uncle Hassan failed to return to his former self. Whenever he regained consciousness, he asked me what date it was. As days went by, his mental strength diminished. So did his body. He said that he craved mutton pasanda. He said there were people dressed in white. I hemmed and hawed and said that they were just doctors and nurses.

He waited for November 10th. That day had no meaning for me, but it was an important day for him, a day to cherish the memory of a great figure. When his mind was clear, he revealed what I wanted to know. He touched with his finger the spot where he assumed the scar under my collarbone was. His finger was warm. The scar where history was imprinted pulsed under his finger.

"I knew it as soon as I saw it. What the scar was . . . The scar is proof of a gunshot. It couldn't have been made with anything else."

"If you say a gunshot, do you mean that a bullet was stuck in here?"

Uncle Hassan nodded heavily. His dry lips opened and a metallic cough drifted out. "You'll know someday. Who gave you the scar."

I tried to remember the person who'd shot me. I couldn't. But I knew that he must have shot my mother and father, too.

After a slight pause, I said, "If I meet him, he sure will get it from me."

"Before you take revenge, time will forgive him. Time tends to be cruel."

He didn't elaborate whether I should forgive him or whether whatever I did would be pointless.

He plunged into a coma that night, but he was briefly lucid in the morning. He asked, "What date is it today?"

"November 10th." It was still October.

"Good. . . . Call me Father."

I was quiet for a few seconds. "Aren't you embarrassed? You're too old to be my father."

"So you don't want to do it?"

"Who said I didn't want to?"

"You want to do it then?"

"Who said I wanted to?"

"You rascal! God bless you."

"Thank you, Father."

"That's all?"

"What?"

"You said thank you and that's it?"

"What else do you want? If you want to be embarrassed, I can say this: Let us meet again in our next lives."

"Ah, did you forget? That we promised the same thing in our previous lives."

"Hah! Just be content that you became a father at your age."

"That's not enough. I was always thirsty. My heart seemed to burn because of the thirst. I feel just like that now. Son, kiss me . . . Yes, that's a good boy . . . I love you."

"I love you, too."

He was silent.

"Did you hear me? I love you. . . . I said I love you!"

I felt my adoptive father's blood flowing into my body. It was warm. I intuited at the moment that all human memories were handed down simply and honestly like this. In the future, I would hand down my adoptive father's blood, not mine, to my children. The imam, who was sitting in a corner, came over and hugged me. That day, I made up my mind to adopt the world.

Exactly at 9:05 on the morning of November 10th that year, I cherished the memory of Ataturk, the hero of Turkish independence, on behalf of Uncle Hassan. I went to the mosque by myself for the first time. Few people were around. The mosque, revealing its white body in what looked like a crater at the heart of the hilly neighborhood, was bouncing off the cool sunlight of late autumn.

Yujong, sitting on the stairs leading to the mosque, was looking down at the city. I knew that he'd been visiting this spot every day. His mother was still missing. The pigeons lurking in every gap at the mosque were his messengers. It wouldn't do him any good even if he understood pigeon speech until he finished crossing the desert, across which no message could be delivered.

I took off my shoes and entered the mosque. I stood facing the mihrab that indicates the direction for prayers, and tried to picture Uncle Hassan praying. I couldn't bring up the image of him praying, although I'd seen him doing it day after day. I had no choice but to pray in my own way. I made a big Korean-style bow. May this bowing not offend Uncle Hassan's God!

As I gazed at the soft sunlight welled in the mosque, I knew that in the future I'd clearly look back at this moment. This snapshot would be summoned from the past and reenacted in whatever manner it might be and at whatever moment it might be. Some meanings would be chipped away and disappear while other meanings would be added. Through a recomposition, this moment would find its way in my past. All things in the present are impetuses toward the future.

My adoptive father's blood is still flowing in my body.

About the Author and the Translator

Sohn Hong-Kyu was born in Jeongup, South Korea, in 1975, and graduated from Dongguk University, majoring in Korean language and literature. He debuted in 2001 with a newcomer's award of the Writers' World. He has a number of short stories and novels to his credit. He has never visited Greece and Turkey, but while writing this novel, he immersed himself in the fictional worlds of Nikos Kazantzakis and Aziz Nesin, as translated into Korean.

Yu Young-Nan is a literary translator living in Seoul. She has translated many Korean novels and short stories into English, most recently Jung Mi-kyung's *My Son's Girlfriend* (2013, Dalkey Archive Press). Her works include Yom Sang-seop's *Three Generations* (2005, Archipelago Books) and Yi In-hwa's *The Everlasting Empire* (2002, Eastbridge), with which she won the 2002 Daesan Foundation Prize for Outstanding Literary Translation.